Email Deliverability Explained

How To Get Email Into The Inbox

Second Edition

Email Deliverability Explained:
How to get email into the inbox

Second Edition.

Published by Ken O'Driscoll.

ISBN (paperback) 978-1-7395433-0-3

First Edition, May 2017.
Second Edition, September 2023.

Set in Source Sans Pro.

Cover design by Steven Saragian (fireintheminddesign.com).

https://emaildeliverabilityexplained.com/

Printed by Amazon.

For Emily

Trademarks

Disclaimer

Preface

Picture this. You have hit send on your email and stepped away for a well-earned break. But wait. That email that took you time to craft and review – it is not hitting subscribers' mailboxes. How can you figure out what went wrong that prevented the messages reaching their intended destinations?

I have been involved in internet email in general, and email deliverability specifically, for a long time. I have owned a deliverability consultancy practice. I have seen it all and worked with many different types of senders.

Today, to consistently reach inboxes over long periods of time, particularly if you are sending bulk emails, requires knowledge of best practice and technical standards - and an understanding of potential pitfalls and what to monitor. It is like a jigsaw and when you put all those pieces together in the correct sequence, you have something called email deliverability.

In truth, most email deliverability problems are completely avoidable. It is straightforward to consistently reach inboxes: once you understand how modern anti-fraud and anti-spam technologies work, follow the current best practices on how to send email, and understand how to measure your success, you should be able to consistently reach the inbox. That is what this book is about.

About the second edition

When I wrote the first edition of Email Deliverability Explained back in 2017, my motivation was to provide concise and accurate information on the fundamentals of email deliverability. At the time, I owned a deliverability consultancy practice and became dismayed by how fragmented and inconsistent the publicly available information was at the time. Clients came to me with deliverability problems that were caused by following advice on a vendor's website.

The deliverability ecosystem has matured over the years, with vendors keeping their knowledge bases up to date, dedicated deliverability conferences, and the growth of online communities. Searching the internet for specific information on deliverability today, you are less likely to encounter widely out of date or inaccurate information than you would have back in 2017. This second edition is a result of my continued motivation to provide a concise and accurate resource for learning about email deliverability.

This book is for anybody who needs to understand email deliverability in simple and practical terms. You can read it cover to cover or use it as a reference. An extensive index is also included. The book is also supported by a website.

In keeping with the ethos of the first edition, I have tried to keep the book concise. That means it avoids as much as possible discussing specific use cases or historical background as to why things work in a particular way.

The first edition was very well received and led to the development of an accompanying training course. Many readers also contacted me, either to simply express their appreciation, or seeking advice. That reader feedback combined with the discussions during training sessions, formed the basis for the second edition.

Changes

The second edition contains three new chapters. Two of the new chapters (2 and 3) explain the technicalities of how internet email works, and how message filters operate. These chapters aim to create a level playing field for those readers who do not have an email background. The third new chapter (6) is devoted to email validation. This topic was briefly covered in the first edition, but now it gets its own chapter.

All the remaining chapters from the first edition have been updated. Some chapters have more extensive updates and rewrites than others.

The first edition contained many references to actual companies that existed at the time. This was intended to help the reader start their search for a particular type of vendor. Since then, nearly every company mentioned has gone through some type of acquisition or merger process as part of wider industry consolidation. That made the book look dated, even though the information was still relevant and accurate. The second edition avoids this problem by keeping the number of vendors mentioned to the minimum. Instead, the supporting website will now contain the vendor information.

I continue to make myself available to readers and am happy to make personal recommendations or introductions as appropriate. My contact details are listed at the back of the book.

Acknowledgements

First and foremost, I would like to thank my readers, whose kind words and constructive feedback ignited the spark in me to create the second edition. I would also like to thank my friends and colleagues at Upland Software. As always, I would like to thank my wife, Emily, and my mother, Ann, for being the most important people in my life, and a source of constant support – I love you both.

Summary

This book contains 12 chapters, a summary of each one is listed below.

Chapter 1 - Introduction
Frames email deliverability around four principles that guide all the best practices.

Chapter 2 - How Internet Email Works
Explains the basic concepts and technologies behind the workings of internet email. It is one of the new chapters in the second edition.

Chapter 3 - Message Filters and Message Streams
Covers message filters and streams. It explains the different types and purposes of filters. It also explains what message streams are and how they can be used to work with filters.

Chapter 4 - Measuring Email Deliverability
Explains how to measure deliverability to understand if you have a deliverability problem.

Chapter 5 - Blocklists and Spam Traps
Covers the different types of spam blocklists, how you get on and off them, and which ones you should be worried about. Spam traps, and their relationship to blocklists, are also covered.

Chapter 6 - Email Address Validation
Explains how email address validation works, and when to use these services.

Chapter 7 - Bounces and List Hygiene
Covers bounce messages and the importance of keeping your contact list in good order.

Chapter 8 - Domain and IP reputation
Explains how reputation filtering works and how to stay on top of it.

Chapter 9 - Content Filters
Explains how filters that operate on the body of an email work.

Chapter 10 - Engagement Filters
Covers how recipient engagement influences deliverability.

Chapter 11 - Email Authentication
Explains how anti-fraud mechanisms can significantly influence deliverability.

Chapter 12 - Conclusion - Putting the jigsaw together
This very short chapter wraps it all up.

Towards the end of the book, you will find information on the author including contact details and a comprehensive index.

Contents

Preface ..... **v**

About the second edition v
Changes vi

Acknowledgements ..... **viii**

Summary ..... **ix**

Chapter 1 Introduction **5**

What is email deliverability? 5
Core Principles 6
Email and the law 7
Unsolicited commercial email 7

Chapter 2 How Internet Email Works **9**

Email Servers 9
Simple Mail Transfer Protocol 9
SMTP Encryption 11
Closed and Open Relays 11
Email Clients 12
Email Addresses 12
Domain Name System 13
MX records 13
The email message 14
The return-path address 15
File attachments 16
MIME 16

Chapter 3 Message Filters and Message Streams **19**

Filter Actions 19
Filter Purposes 20
Outbound message filtering 21
Mail Streams 22
Keeping streams separate 23
Putting it all together – Mail Providers 24

Chapter 4 Measuring Email Deliverability **27**

Core Deliverability Metrics 27
More detailed metrics 31
Inbox Placement Monitoring 33

Unsubscribe Rate 34

Chapter 5 Blocklists and Spam Traps 37

Realtime Block Lists (RBLs) 37
Spam Traps 38
Delisting from an RBL 39
Important RBLs 40
Monitoring your presence on RBLs 41

Chapter 6 Email Address Validation 43

How they work 43
Uses 45
What are the risks? 47

Chapter 7 Bounces and List Hygiene 49

Bounces 49
SMTP status codes 50
Suppression lists 51
Reducing bounces 52
List hygiene 53

Chapter 8 Domain and IP reputation 57

Domain Reputation 57
IP Reputation 60
Maintaining domain and IP reputation 64
IP certification services 65

Chapter 9 Content Filtering 67

Lexical analysis 67
URL Blocklists 69
Checksum Based Filtering 69
Brand-name based filtering 70
Content checking tools 70

Chapter 10 Engagement Filters 73

Key behaviours 73
Identifying engagement-based filtering 74
Recovering from engagement-based blocking 74
Avoidance 75
Be wary of "fake engagement" services 76

Chapter 11 Email Authentication 79

Overview 79
Forward-confirmed reverse DNS 79
Sender Policy Framework 80
DomainKeys Identified Mail 82
DMARC 84
The DMARC record 84
Brand Indicators for Message Identification 86
Monitoring 86

Chapter 12 Conclusion - Putting the Jigsaw Together............. 89

Official Website 91

About the Author 92

Contact Details.. 93

Index 94

Chapter 1
Introduction

This chapter explains email deliverability in simple terms and outlines the core principles that can influence it. We will also touch on the legal aspects of email, including sending unsolicited emails.

What is email deliverability?

Email deliverability is nothing more than getting your messages into recipient inboxes. Sounds straightforward, yes? It is... if you know the rules. To be successful, you need to comply with various standards and follow best current practices to clearly distinguish yourself from spammers.

Spammers are a big problem for mailbox providers because they consume computing resources and steal from customers via fraudulent emails. Therefore, quality mailbox providers pride themselves on having excellent defences against spam. This has led to a much broader definition of what constitutes spam, far beyond sending legally non-compliant emails. For all intents and purposes, spam is now considered to be any message sent which recipients do not appear to want or will likely do them harm, regardless of how legally compliant it is.

While there is some crossover between email deliverability and the methods email marketers use, they are not identical because deliverability applies to all messages, from marketing to transactional, even including regular person-to-person messages. The strategies required to get a bulk promotional campaign delivered to inboxes are often not transferable to identifying why "password reset" messages are being marked as spam. Understanding email deliverability enables you to identify why multiple types of messages may not be reaching inboxes.

Core Principles

Email deliverability is comprised of four core principles:

- Permission
- Engagement
- Reputation
- Compliance

All the standards and best practices fall within one of these principles.

Permission

Modern message filters analyse how recipients treat the messages which they receive. If sufficient recipients of a marketing campaign mark a message as spam, then the filters may consider the whole campaign unwanted and start to mark all messages from that source as spam. Unsolicited messages have a much higher probability of generating complaints, since the recipients were not expecting them in the first place. For email marketers, this means gaining explicit permission from the subscriber that they want to receive your messages. For transactional senders, this means not sending unnecessary notifications to your customers, and giving them the option to switch off specific notifications.

Engagement

Some message filters base their decisions on an analysis of how many recipients interact with and react to your messages. This typically means that if you are sending messages that most recipients do not open, mark as spam, or delete without reading, then all your messages may be filtered as spam.

Reputation

Many message filters take the overall reputation of a sender into account. This involves querying public and private databases to see if the sender has a history of delivering poor quality messages and analysing if the sender appears to be a spammer, based on their technical setup.

Compliance

Being a good sender means complying with various technical standards and guidelines. This is where senders most often trip up because they are often unaware of their compliance obligations.

The four principles above form a guiding light when it comes to deliverability. Do not forget, every element which influences deliverability falls under at least one of the principles.

Email and the law

Most jurisdictions have regulations and laws governing the sending of unsolicited or bulk email. Most also have laws around how you can collect and store contact information.

This book does not cover the legal aspects of commercially sending email messages or the associated data protection requirements. However, you do need to be aware of these issues and be compliant with the relevant legislation. While message filters do not concern themselves with the legality of your messages, recipients can and do make complaints to regulatory bodies. The potential legal and financial implications of not complying with bulk email or data protection requirements can be significant.

In short, if you get permission before sending, never buy or sell contact information, and protect your customer data from theft, you should remain on the right side of most legislation. Always seek legal advice if you are in doubt or do not understand the legislation you are required to comply with.

Unsolicited commercial email

Most commercial email legislation permits businesses to send certain types of unsolicited email. Consequently, many businesses think that just because it is legal, it is an acceptable practice and will automatically result in email reaching the inbox. It's not that simple really, and most legal unsolicited emails end up in spam folders because enough recipients do not want it, so they mark it as spam.

This chapter introduced the concept of email deliverability, which means adhering to standards and following best practices to reach the inbox. The four principles of email deliverability are permission, engagement, reputation, and compliance. All the best practices around deliverability can be categorised under one of these principles. Sending email messages is covered by laws which you need to understand and comply with.

Chapter 2
How Internet Email Works

This chapter explains the basic concepts and technologies behind the workings of internet email. In order to understand deliverability, it is necessary to understand how email works. The chapter refers to both the technical and common terms for many components. Using the correct technical terms when discussing a deliverability problem will often save a lot of time.

Email is a decentralised messaging service which runs over the internet. It is decentralised because it is not centrally operated or controlled by any single organisation or vendor. To participate in internet email, you need access to an email server.

Email Servers

Email messages are sent and received over the internet by Message Transfer Agents (MTAs). An MTA is email server software like Microsoft Exchange, HCL Domino or Postfix. Large mailbox providers such as Google and Yahoo! often write their own MTA software. MTAs are rarely deployed alone. Typically, they are paired with other software, such as spam filters, and hardware, such as network storage for user mailboxes. This book uses the term email server when referring to an MTA by itself and the term email system when referring to the greater infrastructure.

Simple Mail Transfer Protocol

Email servers use a protocol (a set of standard rules) called the Simple Mail Transfer Protocol (SMTP) when communicating with each other. Using the SMTP protocol allows different email servers from different software vendors to understand each other. When two email servers speak SMTP to each other, it is often referred to as an *SMTP conversation*.

During an SMTP conversation, the sending server will transmit a series of commands. The receiving server will respond to each command with a numeric status code.
For example, the SMTP status code of 250 tells the sending server that the last command they issued was accepted without error.

In the following example of the beginning of an SMTP conversation, the sending email server *mta.example.com* wants to deliver a message from *jack@example.com* to *jill@hill.example*, on the receiving email server *mta.hill.example*.

Sender	**SMTP**
mta.hill.example	`220 mta.hill.example SMTP Ready`
mta.example.com	`HELO mta.example.com`
mta.hill.example	`250 mta.hill.example Hello mta.example.com [192.168.10.10], pleased to meet you`
mta.example.com	`MAIL FROM:<jack@example.com>`
mta.hill.example	`250 jack@example.com... Sender ok`
mta.example.com	`RCPT TO:<jill@hill.example>`
mta.hill.example	`250 jill@hill.example. Recipient ok`

In this example, the receiving email server uses the reply code "250" when an SMTP command is accepted, such as when the message is accepted for delivery. Sometimes, the receiving email server is not able to accept the message for delivery. When this happens, it tells the sending email server in the SMTP conversation by using a code other than "250", often called an error code. SMTP error codes can provide useful information when identifying deliverability problems and are covered in detail in Chapter 7.

SMTP Encryption

Originally the internet connections between email servers were not encrypted. This meant that anybody could eavesdrop on the SMTP conversation and see the contents of the messages being transmitted. These days, most email servers support opportunistic encryption, meaning that the SMTP conversation starts out unencrypted until one server asks to upgrade and use encryption. This allows for older email servers and SMTP-aware devices, which do not support encryption, to still participate in internet email.

Internet connections are typically encrypted using the Transport Layer Security (TLS) protocol. The SMTP command STARTTLS is used to start encryption. SMTP-level encryption is a server-to-server process and is completely invisible to email recipients. It is important to understand that STARTTLS only provides protection from eavesdroppers when messages are being transmitted between servers, and not after they have been accepted for delivery.

It is best current practice for email servers to use STARTTLS when possible. Some email clients, including Gmail's webmail, mark messages as "insecure" if they originate from email servers which do not support STARTTLS.

Deliverability problems can occur when email servers have problems negotiating an encrypted connection. This is usually caused by a configuration setting on one of the email servers.

Closed and Open Relays

Email servers will typically only send (relay) messages on behalf of users that they know. For example, an email server managing email for an organisation would only allow employees of that organisation to send emails out through that server. This is typically achieved by requiring users to authenticate themselves before a message can be sent. This arrangement is referred to as a "closed relay" and is the most common instance you will encounter.

However, when an email server relays messages for anybody, without requiring them to authenticate themselves first, it is referred to as an "open relay". Open relays were common in the early days of the internet, until abuse by spammers caused the practice to cease. These days, open relays are usually the result of a misconfiguration and are not intentional. An open relay can cause significant deliverability problems as it can impact the sending reputation of the legitimate sending domain. For more information on sender reputation, see Chapter 8.

Email Clients

People read, send, and interact with email messages through Mail User Agent (MUA) software. Examples of MUAs include Microsoft Outlook, HCL Notes, Apple Mail, and Mozilla Thunderbird. MUAs can also be webmail-based systems like Gmail or mobile apps like the Outlook app. This book uses the terms email client or webmail when referring to an MUA.

To send messages, an email client must connect to an email server. This is still true in the case of webmail; it is just that the presence of the email server is not obvious to the user.

There are several ways an email client can connect to an email server, the most common being the Internet Message Access Protocol (IMAP), the Post Office Protocol (POP), and the Messaging Application Programming Interface (MAPI). Both IMAP and POP have always been open standards meaning that, like SMTP, they are easy to implement since their specifications are public. MAPI was originally developed by Microsoft specifically for use with its email servers. While the MAPI specification has subsequently been published, it is still mainly used to talk to Microsoft software.

The IMAP and POP protocols are only intended for accessing messages, not sending them. Email clients that support POP or IMAP must also support SMTP for sending messages to the email server. MAPI supports both sending and receiving messages.

The TLS protocol is typically used to encrypt connections between email clients and email servers.

Email Addresses

An internet email address is used to identify the message recipient. Email addresses have two parts; the local part which is on the left-hand side of the "@" symbol, and the domain part which is on the right-hand side of the "@" symbol.

Email servers use the domain part of the address to find out which email server is responsible for the recipient. They use the Domain Name System (DNS) to achieve this.

Domain Name System

The Domain Name System (DNS) is used to identify resources on the internet, such as domain names and the services associated with them. Name Servers (NSs), commonly called "DNS servers" run special software which allows them to answer queries for the resources associated with any domains which they manage.

Domain names typically have two or more DNS servers associated with them, all containing identical information. Having more than one DNS server is best current practice in cases where a single server may fail. Remember, if a domain does not have any working DNS, then most internet services associated with the domain, including email, will stop working.

DNS servers store information about resources within Resource Records (RRs). RRs are commonly referred to as DNS records and this book will follow that convention. Different DNS record types are used to label different types of information. For example, the MX record is used to list mail servers responsible for a domain.

MX records

The MX DNS record type specifies a mail exchanger, which is another way of saying the email server which handles incoming messages for the domain.

An MX record contains the name of the email server and its preference. The preference is a numeric value between zero and 65,535, which indicates the order or priority the email server will be tried. MX preference is ordered, with the server having a preference of 1 tried before the sever with a preference of 2, and so on.

Preference	Server
10	mail-01.example.com
20	mail-02.example.org

In the above example, an email server will try to connect to mail-01.example.com first. If it is unable to connect, it will try to connect to mail-02.example.org.

The purpose of the preference value is so that a domain can have multiple email servers responsible for inbound messages. This was useful in the early days of the internet when connections were unreliable and having a backup MX record reduced the chances of messages being lost or unnecessarily delayed. These days, the preference value is largely historic, however it is still required, even if there is only one email server for the domain. In the case of a single server, the actual preference value does not matter.

MX records for sub-domains

It is possible for a sub-domain to have its own MX records that are different from those that manage inbound messages from the base domain. For example, the domain example.com may have one set of MX records while the sub-domain marketing.example.com may have a completely different set.

Receiving messages without having an MX record

A DNS A record is used to map a name to an IP address. If a domain has no MX records but does have an *A* record, then it may still be able to receive messages. Of course, this will only work if that A record points to an email server which is configured to accept messages on behalf of the domain. There is, however, no guarantee that all sending email servers will honour treating a single A record as equivalent to an MX record. Therefore, it is best current practice to always publish MX records for any domain or sub-domain which is expected to receive email messages.

The email message

Email messages consist of two parts: the message headers and message body. The message headers contain information about the message, such as the sender and the subject. Most message headers are not displayed by email clients because they contain information that is only useful when diagnosing problems. Message headers can be added by both the sending and receiving email servers. The message body contains the actual text of the message along with any file attachments.

Following is an example of a complete email message, including headers.

```
Return-Path: <jack@example.com>
Received: from mta.example.com (mta.example.com.
[192.168.10.10]) by mta.hill.example with SMTP id
123456789ABCDEFG Tue, 23 Aug 2023 18:01:11 +0000
(UTC)
Date: Tue, 22 Aug 2023 18:01:11 +0000 (UTC)
From: Jack Climber <jack@example.com>
Message-ID: HIJKLMNOP987654321@example.com
Subject: Hill climb
To: jill@hill.example

Hey Jill,

Are we still climbing that hill on Sunday?

Jack.
```

Common messages headers include *To, From, Subject, Reply-To, Date, Message-ID, and Return-Path.*

The return-path address

One of the most useful message headers is the Return-path header. This header contains the address supplied in the MAIL FROM command during the SMTP conversation. This address is used as a point of contact for the receiving email server in the event of a problem delivering the message to the recipient. The return-path address may be different from the normal From address but does not have to be. Messages sent from the receiving server that are sent to the return-path address are called bounce messages, which are discussed in Chapter 7.

Some other names for the return-path address include the MAIL FROM address, the 5321.MAILFROM, the bounce address, and envelope header.

The visible From address, which the recipient sees and is supplied after the DATA command during the SMTP conversation, is often referred to as the 5322.From address in technical discussions. This is to ensure that everyone knows exactly what From address is being discussed.

> **Note:** The 5221 and 5322 numbers refer to RFCs 5321 and 5322, the specifications which define both the return-path and visible From headers respectively.

This book refers to the return-path and several other specific message headers, so it is important that you know where to find them. Most email clients will allow you to view the complete headers and body of a message. However, it is not always obvious how, so reading the manual or on-line help may be needed.

File attachments

Many computer files, such as word processing documents, are stored as binary files. To send these binary files in email messages, they must first undergo a process of binary-to-text conversion. This is because the SMTP protocol only supports transmitting messages which contain printable ASCII (text) characters. Once the binary file is converted to text by the sender's email client, it can be included in the body of the message. The recipient's email client reverses the process and converts the text attachment back to the original binary format.

There are many ways to perform binary-to-text encoding. The more common ways are called Base64 and uuencode. Unless you are dealing with legacy computer systems or mainframes, you can assume that modern email clients will be able to decode any attachments they receive.

When an email client encodes a binary file, it includes information on what encoding mechanism it used. The receiver's email client then uses this information to decode the attachment and restore the file to its original binary format.

MIME

The need for messages to be able to include file attachments, html formatted text, and non-standard characters all in the same message led to the development of the Multipurpose Internet Mail Extensions (MIME). MIME provides a standardised way for different types of content to be included in the same email message. MIME is implemented on email clients not servers, meaning that you need to have a MIME-capable email client to read or send MIME messages. This is less of a concern today as it was when MIME was first developed. These days, it is difficult to find an email client that does not support MIME.

MIME is typically invisible to message recipients. If MIME has been implemented incorrectly however, then the message may appear garbled or not display at all. Programmers writing software which send email messages should become familiar with the details of the MIME standard.

These days most internet messages are MIME messages.

This chapter explained the basics of internet email. Email servers (MTAs) send messages to each other over the internet, using the SMTP protocol. SMTP error codes can be used for troubleshooting. SMTP conversations between email servers are commonly encrypted using TLS. Email clients (MUAs) are connected to email servers and used for reading and composing messages. Email clients talk to email servers using protocols such as SMTP, IMAP, POP, and MAPI.

When an email server has messages for a domain, it looks up the DNS MX records to see the address of the email server responsible for that domain. It is possible that a sub-domain can have different MX records than the base domain.

Email messages are made up of the headers and the body. The headers contain information added by both the sending and receiving servers and are useful for troubleshooting.

Email clients convert binary files to text files before sending them. The MIME standard is the most common format for messages today. MIME allows for a single message to include multiple types of content, such as html text or non-printable characters.

Chapter 3
Message Filters and Message Streams

This chapter covers message filters and streams. It explains the different types and purposes of filters. It also explains what message streams are and how they can be used to work with filters.

Message filters are specialist pieces of software designed to classify messages and decide if they reach their intended destination, for example a recipient's inbox, or not. A filter can be a software application which is installed on an email server, a dedicated hardware appliance, or built-in to an email client. To learn more about email servers and clients, see Chapter 2. Message filters can also be hosted on the internet and provided as a service.

Filter Actions

Message filters can perform several actions on email messages.

1. Move the message somewhere other than the inbox, such as the "spam" folder or a quarantine area.

2. Modify the subject of the message. For example, by prefixing "SPAM" or "EXTERNAL" to the original subject.

3. Add a special message header, such as the results of email authentication checks. For more information on email authentication, see Chapter 11.

4. Refuse to deliver the message. This typically causes a bounce message to be generated. For more information on bounces, see Chapter 7.

5. Silently delete the message.

The action a filter takes is determined by the individual filter configuration. The default settings of most filters will not silently delete messages; the filter must be specifically configured to do so by the user.

Filter Purposes

Message filters have four main purposes - security, spam, authentication and compliance.

Security

Security filters look for attachments and other message content which may pose a risk to the recipient. These filters often look for computer viruses and malicious software (malware). Sometimes, security filters will follow the links in messages and scan the websites they are pointing to. Following links can cause issues with "open rate" metrics, this is explained in Chapter 4.

Spam

Spam filters look for signals which indicate that the message is potentially spam. These filters are often based on a scoring system. Each spam signal increases the score until the threshold is reached, and the message is presumed to be spam. Of course, some signals can increase the score such that their presence alone can cause a message to be marked as spam.

The many different types of spam filtering technologies are explained in the coming chapters.

Blocklists	Chapter 5
Domain and IP Reputation	Chapter 8
Content	Chapter 9
Engagement (recipient behaviour)	Chapter 10

Spam Filter False Positives

Sometimes, a spam filter makes a mistake and marks a non-spam message as spam. This is called a false positive. False positives can occur for many reasons from poorly maintained filtering software to a message having too many similarities to previously detected spam. For more information on false positives related to similar looking messages, see

Checksum Based Filtering in Chapter 9. Information on contacting providers to report false positives is provided later in this chapter.

When a spam filter does not detect a spam message and lets it through, it is known as a false negative. For spam filter software to be considered reliable, it must have consistently low false positive and false negative rates. Not every organisation operates reliable spam filters. For this reason, false positives are a possibility that must be kept in mind when diagnosing deliverability problems.

Authentication / Policy

Authentication filters investigate whether a message conforms to certain email authentication technical standards. Email authentication is covered in Chapter 11.

Compliance

Compliance filters look for specific message content, or other properties related to the compliance rule they are tasked with enforcing. For example, a compliance filter may be set to block customers from emailing credit card numbers to the billing department. These filters are usually used to enforce regulatory compliance. The specific filtering rules are determined by the organisation using the filter. Such filters are common in financial, pharmaceutical, and other regulated industries. Resolving problems caused by compliance filters typically involves removing the offending content from your messages or contacting the organisation directly to respectfully request that your messages bee allowed through.

Outbound message filtering

When dealing with email deliverability it is common to think that only the recipient's email system has message filters. After all, it is typically the recipient who will claim they never received a message, or it was received but landed in the spam folder. While it is true that many deliverability issues relate to the recipient's email system, that is not always the case.

Message filters also exist on the sender's email system to scan their outbound messages. It is common for mailbox providers and corporations to do their best to block their users from sending messages with viruses attached. Corporate email systems will often additionally use compliance filters to scan outbound messages. For example, some compliance filters restrict what type of files can be attached to outbound messages.

When diagnosing a deliverability issue, always ensure that the message left the sender's email system first. This can usually be achieved by looking at the logs on the sending email server.

Mail Streams

A typical organisation may send out many different types of messages. For example, they may send out a newsletter to all their customers, replies to customer support tickets, and send general correspondence. Many message filters divide these different types of messages into categories, often referred to as mail streams. The most common mail streams are:

Regular / one-to-one

Regular messages are typically personal, or business messages sent over a day or series of days. They are not sent in bulk and only to a single or small number of recipients. They are also sent from an address associated with a person, and not a role account such as sales@example.com. Regular messages typically receive replies and are sent to recipients who may have the sender address stored in their contact lists.

Transactional

Transactional messages are associated with fulfilling a service. Examples of transactional messages include electronic invoices, support ticket updates, and password reset instructions. They are typically sent from an address associated with a role, and not an individual. Many transactional messages are time sensitive and need to be delivered as soon as possible.

Marketing

Marketing messages are promotional in nature. Examples of marketing messages include newsletters, new product announcements, and abandoned cart notifications.

Keeping streams separate

The more advanced message filters, especially those operated by large receivers, often treat different message streams differently. For example, a spam filter may be designed to be more lenient with bulk messages that look transactional in nature while scrutinising others more closely. This is common sense as recipients are not particularly tolerant of password reset messages landing in spam, for whatever reason. Likewise, individual messages may be treated differently to bulk messages, even if they have the same content. For this reason, it is always a good idea for a sender to clearly distinguish different mail streams, both by content and sending means.

The most important way you can use content to distinguish streams, is to never mix transactional and marketing content in the same message. For example, including a special offer in a password reset notification may cause the message to be considered as marketing related. This could result in it being treated differently, such as with delayed delivery.

Traditionally, the recommended method for technically distinguishing different streams was to send them from different IP addresses. These days, while it will not do any harm, the use of dedicated IPs is not nearly as important as it was.

A good way to distinguish different streams is to use different DomainKeys Identified Mail (DKIM) signing domains on each stream. For more information on DKIM, see Chapter 11.

Another method of distinguishing streams is to use different sub-domains for each stream. For example, newsletter@email.example.com and sales@crm.example.com. Using different sub-domains will help segment domain reputation between the two domains, which can help limit deliverability problems. For more information on domain reputation, see Chapter 8.

Putting it all together – Mail Providers

Maintaining a reliable email system can be expensive and time consuming. It is for this reason that most organisations outsource some or all their email requirements to third parties. The most common third parties that manage email on behalf of organisations are Email Service Providers, Mailbox Providers, and hosted software solutions.

Email Service Providers

Email Service Providers (ESPs) have email systems which are designed to send high volumes of email messages very quickly. They typically offer additional services, such a web interface to create and track the success of email campaigns. ESPs may also record bounce messages (see Chapter 7) and complaints.

There are many different types of ESP. For example, some ESPs focus purely on marketing messages, while others include social media messaging features. There are also ESPs which specialise in sending transactional messages.

Specialist ESPs also exist to service niches. For example, some ESPs specialise in sending bulk messages for non-profit organisations.

Mailbox Providers

Originally, Internet Service Providers (ISPs) bundled email services along with connections to the internet. Over time other organisations began to offer email services too. This book uses the term Mailbox Provider (MBP) when referring to both traditional ISPs and newer providers.

They typically offer message sending, receiving, storage, and filtering services. Others may also offer hosted address book and calendar features.

MBPs typically do not intend their services to be used for sending large volumes of messages and may even suspend users who attempt to do so. To send bulk messages properly, you need an ESP.

Many MBPs use message filters which make decisions based on the volume of complaints associated with a particular sender. If enough recipients use the "report spam" option, it can hurt deliverability by causing all your email to go straight to the spam folder.

Some MBPs provide feedback to senders on recipients that mark messages as spam. They do this via Feedback Loops (FBLs). FBLs are an automated way for mailbox providers to report information on complaints back to the sending ESP. The ESP will typically present this information to their users on a dashboard along with other metrics.

Larger MBPs, such as Yahoo! and Microsoft operate their own FBL service. Other providers offer FBLs via a third-party service operated by a company called Validity.

Google does not provide a traditional FBL service. To use Google's FBL a sender must include a special message header in their bulk messages. Google provides aggregate data on the number of complaints via their Google Postmaster Tools service.

Larger MBPs often provide a way for senders to contact them in cases where they believe that their messages are being filtered incorrectly. This is commonly referred to as "contacting the Postmaster".

Hosted Software

Hosted software, often referred to as Software as a Service (SaaS), is software which is delivered over the internet. For example, the Customer Relationship Management (CRM) software provided by Salesforce, the accounting software provided by Xero, and the Calendly calendar booking tool are all hosted software solutions.

Hosted software solutions can either send through an organisation's existing MBP, use a third-party ESP, or use their own email systems.

Self-hosted email systems

Some organisations do not outsource their email and instead use commercial or open-source email systems which they install and maintain themselves. It is very difficult to diagnose deliverability problems with these email systems since it cannot be known how the message filters have been configured.

It is important to choose the right mail provider for the type of messages you intend to send. Not doing so can result in deliverability challenges which are avoidable. For example, do not use a mailbox provider for sending bulk marketing messages.

This chapter covered message filters and mail streams. Message filters can scan, re-direct and even delete messages before they reach the inbox. Filters typically scan for security risks such as viruses, spam, and problems with email authentication. Organisation-specific filters can also scan for prohibited words and phrases specific to that organisation's policies. Filters can treat different message streams differently. Transactional messages such as password-resets may be treated more leniently than marketing messages. It is best practice not to mix transactional and marketing content in the same message. You can use different sub-domains and DKIM signing to differentiate message streams. There are different types of mail providers for different message streams. It is important to choose the right provider for your content. For example, you should use an ESP for sending bulk messages and not an MBP.

Chapter 4
Measuring Email Deliverability

This chapter explains how you can measure email deliverability, both broadly and precisely.

You cannot hope to improve or maintain your deliverability unless you can first measure its current position. Measuring deliverability will allow you to identify problems as soon as they occur and sometimes even before! Measurement will also allow you to monitor the effects of technical and content changes you make to the messages you are sending.

There are three core metrics which can be used to measure any type of scenario where you send messages out, be that regular business messages, a marketing campaign, or transactional messages from a web application. Once you know you have a problem, you can then apply more precise measurements depending on the type of messages you are sending.

The metrics used to measure deliverability are not always the same as those used to measure the success of an email marketing campaign. So, while there may be some crossover, keep in mind that measuring deliverability and measuring email campaign success are two different undertakings.

Core Deliverability Metrics

The three-core metrics used to measure email deliverability are:

1. Delivery rate
2. Bounce rate
3. Complaint rate

These three metrics can be used to measure email deliverability for any email activity.

Delivery Rate

The delivery rate is the total percentage of messages which were accepted by mailbox providers.

To calculate the delivery rate, you need to know the quantity of messages sent and the number of bounced messages.

$$\frac{Total\ Messages\ Sent - Total\ Bounces}{Total\ Messages\ Sent} * 100$$

Delivery rate should usually be a high number. A ninety eight percent or higher delivery rate signifies healthy email deliverability.

If the number of messages sent is considerably greater than the number of messages accepted, that can indicate problems with invalid email addresses or blocking by messages filters.

The delivery rate simply measures how many messages were received by mailbox providers; not how many were filtered away from the inbox following receipt.

To measure regular outgoing business emails, the delivery rate is a useful metric. Combined with clients and suppliers reporting that your mail is going into their spam folders, you can quickly see if you have a problem.

For marketing campaigns and transactional messages, the delivery rate needs to be combined with the complaint and bounce rates to provide more relevant information.

Bounce Rate

The bounce rate is the percentage of sent messages for which recipient mailboxes either refused to accept or accepted, then later sent a bounce message. A bounce message means that the message did not reach the recipient.

To calculate the bounce rate, you need to know the total number of messages sent, and the total number of bounces received.

$$\frac{Total\ Bounces\ Received}{Total\ Messages\ Sent} * 100$$

Ideally a bounce rate should be between zero and two percent. A high bounce rate indicates that you may have a problem.

Bounce messages also have a very useful feature. They often tell you exactly *why* the message did not reach the recipient. For example, receiving lots of bounces saying "Invalid address" may indicate that you are sending to invalid addresses and should review your data quality.

ESPs typically report the bounce rate of individual campaigns as standard. Many also break down the reasons for the bounces and categorise the information on a per-mailbox provider basis. This level of detail can be very useful in isolating a deliverability problem.

The bounce rate should always be monitored, since a consistently high bounce rate is both a sign of a deliverability problem and it may damage your sending reputation if not corrected.

Bounce messages, including the most common reasons for them, are covered in Chapter 7. Sending reputation is covered in Chapter 8. Along with bounces, complaints should also be closely monitored.

Complaint Rate

The complaint rate is the percentage of complaints received in response to your email activity. Recipients usually complain about messages which are unexpected, unwanted, or both. They can either contact you directly to complain or mark your message as spam in their email client. If they are very angry, they may do both!

To calculate the complaint rate, you need to know the total number of messages sent, and the total number of complaints received.

$$\frac{FBL\ Complaints + Direct\ Complaints}{Total\ Messages\ Sent} * 100$$

A small number of complaints is normal and nothing to worry about. People sometimes forget that they subscribed to a list or think marking a message as spam is just a way to get it out of the inbox.

A high number of complaints is a sign that there is a problem with your messages or recipients. This often leads to deliverability problems. Ideally, you want to keep your complaint rate below one percent.

When a recipient contacts you directly to complain, remove them from your list, politely let them know and move on, regardless of the merits of their complaint. Ensure that you are monitoring your abuse@ mailbox (see Chapter 8). If a recipient does not feel that contacting you directly is working, they will often contact your ESP.

When a complaint rate is zero and the delivery rate is low, it can indicate large scale blocking across one or more mailbox providers. The complaint rate is zero because all messages are being sent straight to the spam folder, so it has already been marked as spam. Do not take complaint rates personally. While some will be in response to your content, recipients may also mark messages as spam for many other reasons. For example, a recipient may make a mistake, or use “Mark as Junk” as a way to remove messages from their inbox.

The reported complaint rate does not always account for all the recipients that complained. That is because some mailbox providers only report complaints made by their free users, and not those that pay for the service. Be careful with this metric if you primarily send messages to businesses.

More detailed metrics

The three key deliverability metrics are independent of any business model and provide a high-level view of deliverability.

To discover more details about deliverability, additional measurements can be used. Not every measurement is suitable for every business model, so do not try to implement these all at once; they need to make sense for your organisation.

Conversion Rate

The conversion rate is the percentage of recipients who received the message, opened and read it, and took the desired action. The desired action can be anything from booking an appointment to purchasing a product to making a reservation. The desired action can occur offline and does not have to involve clicking a link in the email.

Be careful not to confuse conversion rate with click through rate, which simply measures recipients clicking on links within the message (see next section).

The ideal conversion rate is specific to an individual business. Typically, a low conversion rate can often indicate problems with the message copy or audience alignment. And that is something you should address with your marketing colleagues!

Click through rate

The click through rate is the percentage of recipients who clicked on one or more links in the message.

Unless the desired action occurs offline (for example, a telephone call), this metric is directly related to the conversion rate. A high click through rate and a low conversion rate often indicates a problem with marketing message and value alignment between the email and the website landing page. It can also indicate a technical issue which prevents the recipient from easily following through on the desired action.

Click through rate is tracked by your Email Service Provider (ESP). Once enabled, all the links in the email are replaced with special tracking links. When a recipient clicks a tracking link, they are taken to the landing page after the click is recorded.

The presence of tracking links themselves can cause deliverability problems due to the reputation of the tracking domain the ESP use. Using your own domain in the tracking link, as discussed in Chapter 7, helps minimise this risk.

Open Rate

The open rate is the percentage of recipients who open the message after it has been received.

Open rate is tracked using a web beacon, which is a unique invisible image (measuring 1x1 pixels) which is linked to the specific email message. It is loaded when the recipient opens the email - just like any other remote image, except it is not visible to the human eye. When a web beacon is loaded, it is recorded, and the information associated with the individual recipient. Open rate is typically tracked by your ESP.

In the past, open rate was a relatively reliable metric. It is increasingly becoming less reliable as it depends on the recipient automatically loading images in their email. In recent years, images which are loaded remotely in email messages are increasingly seen as an invasion of recipient privacy. Consequently, some mailbox providers, email clients, and message filters are taking steps to stop web beacons from working entirely. These steps include disabling the loading of remote images by default for senders who are not listed in the recipient's contacts. Some providers will block the individual opens, and instead report simulated opens based on aggregate results.

Because of this, open rate is no longer a reliable deliverability metric, and it should be used with caution. However, it can still be a useful metric once you understand its limitations. A sudden drop in open rates can indicate problems with messages reaching inboxes.

Both open and click through metrics are especially vulnerable to false positives caused by security filters.

Security filters and open metrics

Some security filters will follow the links in messages to see where they go. This is intended to protect recipients by ensuring that links in messages do not lead to malicious websites. However, this well-intentioned activity, often referred to as "bot clicks", can cause false positives with any metric based on messages being opened or links clicked. You can normally identify bot clicks by looking for improbably large numbers of opens or clicks registering in the first few minutes of a campaign being sent. Bot clicks often originate from IP networks associated with data centres and not corporate or home internet connections. Many ESPs have developed ways to suppress bot clicks from their metric dashboards.

Inbox Placement Monitoring

Inbox placement monitoring reports the percentage of recipients who received the messages directly to their inbox and filtered to another folder by the mailbox provider. This type of monitoring will show how many messages were delivered but ended up in spam folders. For recipients using Gmail as their mailbox provider, this metric also measures messages which land in the non-priority inboxes, such as Promotions. This may be an interesting metric to discuss with your marketing colleagues as it could help to explain low open rates.

Inbox placement is tracked by third party services using seed addresses. Seed addresses are test (seed) email accounts with different mailbox providers and behind multiple message filters. To measure inbox placement, these seed email addresses are subscribed to your mailing list or otherwise included in your mail flow. They receive the same messages as your regular recipients, and you receive a report on how many seed email address inboxes received the message. The information is typically broken down by mailbox provider and filter provider. This allows you to see if you have a deliverability problem with a specific provider which can be very useful.

One challenge to seed testing is engagement-based message filtering. These filters change how they respond to messages over time, based on how recipients are interacting with them in real time. This means that a seed test performed before a campaign may not give an accurate indication of how the campaign will perform. One way to reduce this risk is to run tests both before and while a campaign is in the process of sending. Engagement filtering is covered in Chapter 10.

While seed lists are not 100 percent accurate, they do provide a very good understanding of how different mailbox providers and message filter vendors are responding to an email campaign. If a campaign has a high delivery rate but a low inbox rate, this can indicate a problem with the email being classified as spam.

In the past, another type of inbox placement monitoring called panel data was also used. Panel data involved retaining a panel of real people who shared access to their email accounts with the panel data provider, in return for some form of compensation. Some mailbox providers also provided anonymised information on their users' mailbox behaviour in return for a fee. Panel data providers claimed that the service offered the most authentic feedback on how recipients interact with email messages. This may have been true since seed lists are automated and typically do not interact with messages in the same way a regular recipient would. However, there were concerns relating to how recipients consented to their accounts being monitored by a third party. Google was the first provider to discontinue allowing panel data providers access to their systems, regardless of whether a user had given consent or not. Given the market coverage of Google, this proved to be a death blow to the panel data industry of the time. Today, there are still some panel data providers, but they use statistical simulations to emulate the old recipient panels, maintain a panel with very limited mailbox coverage, or use a combination of both.

Unsubscribe Rate

The unsubscribe rate is the percentage of recipients unsubscribing from the mailing list. This is an inaccurate method of measuring engagement. Recipients often ignore unwanted marketing mails over long periods of time, instead of going through the unsubscribe process. However, this metric can sometimes be useful to measure the response to a significant change in the marketing message being communicated within an existing list. In certain situations, an increase in unsubscribes may even indicate a negative emotional response to message content (for example, an unwise attempt at humour). While more a marketing metric, it can be useful to monitor in cases where there is no other obvious reason for a drop in deliverability. Unsubscribe rate is tracked by your email server or your ESP. Bot clicks (discussed previously) can also unintentionally un-subscribe recipients when the unsubscribe link does not require any type of user confirmation.

This chapter covered how to measure email deliverability. The three core deliverability metrics are delivery, bounces, and complaints. They can be used to measure almost anything you will need to measure. More detailed metrics can be used; however, they depend on the type of email you are sending. Detailed metrics include conversions, click throughs, and inbox placement. Some detailed metrics are not very accurate by themselves and should be used alongside other metrics. These less accurate metrics include tracking email opens and list unsubscribes. Bot clicks can distort any metric that is based on opens or link clicks.

Chapter 5
Blocklists and Spam Traps

This chapter covers blocklists, which are a well-established method used to fight spam and a common cause of deliverability problems. The chapter also discusses spam traps, and their relationship to blocklists.

Realtime Block Lists (RBLs)

Realtime Block Lists (RBLs) contain lists of IP addresses, whole IP networks, and domain names, which are considered known sources of spam. They are maintained by various companies, organisations, and individuals. Each RBL has its own listing criteria, or policy on what sending behaviour it takes to get on the list.

Mailbox providers, email servers, and message filters use RBLs to inform their filtering decisions. Typically, when a message is associated with an RBL it is either rejected outright or put into a spam folder.

Many RBLs are free to use, but some are commercial and operate on a paid subscription basis. RBL entries can be specific, such as a domain name or broad, such as an entire IP network.

Even if you are not sending spam, it is still possible for you to be listed by an RBL. This is known as a false positive and can occur for several reasons. For example, sending from an IP address shared with other senders, one of which is a spammer.

Many RBLs use a combination of direct user reports, industry feedback, and data from spam traps to build up their listings of spam sources.

Spam Traps

Spam traps are special email addresses which are designed to detect poor sending habits. There is no valid user behind a spam trap address. RBL operators use spam trap addresses to keep their lists up to date by continuously collecting information on new sources of spam.

Spam trap email addresses typically look like regular addresses. Some organisations even work with RBL operators and create spam traps for them, using the domain name of their organisation and making it next to impossible to detect a spam trap address by simply looking at it.

The three main categories of spam trap are:

1. Recycled traps
2. Pristine traps
3. Typo traps

Recycled traps were once valid addresses which have now been converted into spam traps. The conversion process typically involves the address rejecting all incoming messages for at least twelve months before it begins accepting messages again. Recycled traps are designed to catch senders who do not manage their bounces properly. For more information on bounces, see Chapter 7.

Pristine traps have never been valid addresses. They are often planted on websites in ways that only web scrapers could detect. Pristine traps are designed to catch senders who buy low-quality lists of email addresses that comprise of scraped data.

Typo traps are intentional misspellings of a recipient's domain, such as gmsil.com instead of gmail.com. These traps are designed to catch senders who have low data quality checks and standards.

It's important to remember that spam traps are designed to catch spammers, not legitimate email senders. When a sender gets a spam trap on their list, it is usually down to the way the email address was collected or how the sender manages their list. Buying contact lists or re-engaging with old subscribers who have not been contacted in over twelve months are the two main ways spam traps get on a list.

Detection and Removal

When you experience a sudden drop in deliverability after changing your sending behaviour, it may be the result of a spam trap being contacted. This will in turn cause an RBL listing, which can cause deliverability problems for any receiver which subscribes to that specific RBL.

If you send messages through an Email Service Provider (ESP), they may reach out to you and tell you that you have a spam trap on your list. Third party RBL monitoring tools will alert you to a RBL listing, which, depending on how the RBL operates, may be associated with hitting a spam trap. Email validation services, discussed in Chapter 6, can scan a list for potential spam traps. However, the process may not be one hundred percent accurate, so proceed with caution.

The only absolute way to remove possible spam traps from an email list or affected list segment is to re-confirm the entire list. Reconfirming is the process of asking each contact if they still want to be on the list. Every contact that does not respond must be removed, as they are all now potential spam traps. This is not to be confused with a marketing technique which uses multiple re-confirms to further qualify contacts; this is a once-off 'in or out?' list reconfirmation.

Once a spam trap is removed, or you have identified a way not to send to the segment likely containing the trap again, you need to apply to the RBL operator for delisting.

Delisting from an RBL

RBLs need to be dynamic to be effective. That means that it is in the interest of most RBL operators to ensure that the information they list is accurate. Continuing to list an IP address that is no longer sending spam or listing an IP address that never sent spam decreases the value of the list to those that use it.

Every RBL has a unique method of requesting an entry to be removed. The procedure is usually automated, and instructions can be found on the website associated with the RBL. In general, the de-listing procedure works as follows:

1. You confirm that your IP or domain is listed via a lookup on the RBL operator's site
2. The site explains the reason for the listing
3. If the reason for the listing is that you are reported as a source of spam, or are sending to a spam trap, then you must manage that issue before requesting the delisting
4. When you have managed/handled any issues raised, you request the delisting

Delisting can take anywhere between minutes and days, depending on the list and the internal processes used to verify the request.

It is very important to make certain that your organisation was not a source of spam. Repeated delisting requests without investigating the cause can result in long delays between delistings. Being listed might not be your fault. Since spammers use compromised servers to relay their spam, legitimate senders can become unwitting sources of spam following security breaches, such as a web server being compromised.

Some RBLs use an automatic delisting process. This means that if the RBL does not detect further spam traps from a sender in a certain space of time, the listing is automatically removed.

Static RBLs are the exception to the delisting process, as they only list static IP ranges that rarely change, for example a list of IP addresses associated with home broadband internet. You really do not need to worry about these lists, as you will not be sending from home broadband connections.

Important RBLs

There are hundreds of RBLs. Some are provided by commercial organisations, others operate on a not-for-profit basis, and some are run purely as hobbies.

The only universal RBLs you should care about are those operated by Spamhaus (https://spamhaus.org/). Spamhaus provides multiple lists based on different listing criteria. Being listed by Spamhaus is a problem because it is very widely used by mailbox providers, message filters, and email servers around the world. Getting listed on Spamhaus is guaranteed to cause deliverability problems. Spamhaus often communicates listings to ESPs directly, meaning that your ESP could be aware that you are hitting spam traps, even if you have not realised it yet.

Depending on who you send to, other RBLs which have significant coverage in certain sectors are:

Barracuda (https://www.barracudacentral.org/rbl)
Cloudmark Sender Intelligence (https://csi.cloudmark.com/en/reset)
Invaluement (https://www.invaluement.com/)
NoSolicitado (https://www.nosolicitado.org/)
Proofpoint (https://ipcheck.proofpoint.com/)

Some RBLs are operated on a *grudge* basis. Grudge RBLs are those RBLs which list non-spammer behaviour, which the operator nonetheless considers to be problematic. An example is RBLs that list the IPs of every ESP, or list domains which do not have a website. You can safely ignore being listed on such RBLs as they are not used by any receiver of consequence.

Monitoring your presence on RBLs

Often the first time a sender discovers that they are on an RBL is when they start to see a decline in deliverability.

If you are affected, all the RBLs mentioned in the previous paragraph allow you to query them via their websites. Some online services allow you to query multiple RBLs in one go.

However manually querying RBLs is not very practical. To address this, third party services can automatically monitor RBLs for the presence of your sending IPs and domain names. These services send you an alert the moment a listing is detected. While very useful, you really need to ensure that the service only alerts you to RBLs which you care about. Otherwise, your inbox will become cluttered with useless alerts.

It is always a good idea to check any new IP addresses for listing before they are used to send emails. This is covered in more detail in Chapter 8.

This chapter covered RBLs and spam traps. RBLs list IP addresses and domains which are considered sources of spam and are used by providers to block incoming email. Spam traps are fake email addresses used by RBL operators to identify spammers so that they can include them on their lists. You can engage a third-party service to automatically monitor for your presence on RBLs. Always check new IP addresses against RBLs before using them.

Chapter 6
Email Address Validation

This chapter covers email validation services. It explains what they are, how they work, and when you may need them. The chapter also discusses the risks of using these services.

An email validation service takes a list of addresses and uses various methods to calculate the probability of each address bouncing, being a spam-trap, or having other issues that may prevent delivery. Such services typically provide a means to upload a list of addresses to be validated along with an Application Programming Interface (API) for real-time validation.

How they work

A validation service can use several methods to determine the probability of an address being valid. It is important to understand that these services cannot confirm the validity of any address with one hundred percent accuracy.

Querying the mail server

Historically, the earliest method to assess if an email address was valid was to query the recipient email server directly. The early internet could be described as a world of trust, and internet mail systems were no different. Consequently, early email servers supported the VRFY and EXPN SMTP commands. The VRFY command allowed you to query if a mailbox existed on the server. The EXPN command was used to expand distribution lists, listing the complete email addresses of all list members. For more information on SMTP, see Chapter 2. Support for these commands began to decrease significantly as spammers started to abuse them. Today these commands are no longer supported by most internet email systems.

The second method of querying an email server directly is to pretend to deliver a message. This is achieved by issuing a QUIT command before the DATA command in the SMTP conversation. Many, but not all, mail servers will confirm the validity of the address after the RCPT TO command.

```
MAIL FROM:<bogus_user@validator.example>
250 2.1.0 Ok
RCPT TO:<invalid.address@example.com>
550 5.1.1 <invalid.address@example.com>: Recipient
address rejected: User unknown
QUIT
221 2.0.0 Bye
```

Pretending to deliver messages is controversial, because, when carried out at scale, it can unnecessarily consume an internet mail system's computational resource. There are also privacy and security considerations with disclosing valid addresses. Therefore, many mailbox providers and email systems take active measures against being probed in this manner.

The other challenge with this approach to validating addresses is that it does not work all the time. Some email systems operate by initially accepting all messages, before deciding what messages are addressed to valid recipients. If the address is found to be invalid, a bounce message is generated. For more information on bounces, see Chapter 7. This type of architecture is deployed by many large organisations and mailbox providers.

Typographical analysis

Analysing email addresses for typographical errors such as common misspelling of domain names is a simple way to identify many potential problems. For example, when filling in a web form, it is not uncommon for users to enter *gmsil.com* instead of *gmail.com*.

Typographical analysis can often achieve a high level of accuracy because the analytics engines that are used have been developed and trained by linguists as opposed to software developers. This is because the science of identifying commonly mis-typed or mis-spelled words has applications far beyond that of verifying email addresses. For example, the same technology is behind the auto-correct feature on software applications.

Buying data

Some Internet Service Providers (ISPs) sell information related to how their customers interact with the email services they provide. This information typically relates to bounces and complaints. For bounces, the data includes their own customer addresses which are no longer valid, and the invalid addresses which their customers attempted to contact. ISP complaint data is based on their customers who marked messages as spam within the ISP's own email service.

A few Email Service Providers (ESPs) also sell their bounce and complaint data. The complaint data provided by ESPs covers their customers' recipients who marked messages as spam. ESP complaint data is taken from Feedback Loops (FBLs) which contain the complainant's email address data. For more information on FBLs, see Chapter 3.

Some data brokers will also sell information on invalid addresses that their customers report to them as being invalid after buying access to contact details.

This practice of selling user data is controversial and typically limited to jurisdictions with weaker consumer data privacy laws. This can influence the effectiveness of a validation service on email addresses belonging to residents of more privacy-focused jurisdictions.

Data analytics

A verification service with a sufficiently large collection of accumulated email addresses can analyse that data to determine the probability of addresses being valid or not. One way to achieve this is to look at historical frequency of how many times an address was submitted for validation, and the overall profile of the customers submitting the address. For example, if an address is seen to be frequently submitted with the same known invalid addresses, then the probability of it being invalid increases. Data analytics are often combined with other validation methods.

Uses

There are many uses for email validation.

When collecting addresses off-line

When addresses are manually transcribed, such as verbally, over the telephone, or scanned by Optical Character Recognition (OCR) software, there is a margin for error. This typically occurs in scenarios like trade shows or conferences. In this scenario, contact details may be verbally communicated, written on paper forms, or gathered from business cards that are dropped into fishbowls.

Using a validation service, particularly one which supports typographical analysis, can be very helpful in these cases to identify both human and software errors.

When address confirmation is delayed

When people type their email address into on-line forms there is a margin for error. To prevent this, confirming that those addresses did indeed sign up is best current practice. This confirmation is normally achieved by sending a confirmation message to the address. However, it may not always be appropriate to implement confirmation immediately. For example, when registering or signing up for a software trial, validation could be delayed, keeping the process as simple and straightforward as possible. Integrating a validation service API into the sign-up process allows for addresses to be validated in real-time. While recipient-side confirmation is still needed, it can be applied later in the on-boarding process.

Before contacting stale addresses

Email addresses age. There is no guarantee that an email address to which you successfully delivered a message last year, is still valid, or in use by the same person. When you are faced with a mailing list, or segment of a mailing list, which has not been contacted in a while, it is best current practice to carry out a re-confirmation campaign.

When email addresses have not been contacted in nine months or longer, it is a good idea to pass them through a validation service first. This may reduce the number of bounces the campaign will have, which will help protect your sending reputation. For more information on bounces, see Chapter 7.

Removing spam traps

If you have inherited a mailing programme or acquired an email list of unknown quality or age, running the addresses through a validation service will give you an idea of the health of the list by identifying potential spam traps. For more information on spam traps, see Chapter 5.

What are the risks?

Legal

In many jurisdictions there is legislation in place to protect customer and personal data. Email addresses typically fall into that category. In some jurisdictions, email addresses may be considered Personally Identifiable Information (PII). Purchasing or renting an email list does not automatically exempt you from these laws.

When you give an email address that does not belong to you to a third party such as a validation service, you need to be sure that they will afford that data all the protections required by the jurisdiction(s) you are operating in. In some cases, you may need to comply with the laws of the jurisdiction that the owner of the email address belongs to.

Especially when using an API to validate email addresses in real time, it is often easy to forget that you are transferring data to a third party. Therefore, it is important to consult legal counsel and fully understand your legal obligations before engaging a validation service.

Not understand the limitations

Validating email addresses is not an exact process and there is a margin of error. Some providers are up front and honest about this, others less so. For example, many providers will report addresses that are managed by mail servers which accept all messages initially as being "unverifiable". While technically correct, this does not mean that the addresses are invalid, just that pretending to deliver messages to them does not work.

Reputational risk

The email validation sector has a disproportionate number of disreputable operators who will pretend to validate your email addresses, while in practice sell them on to spammers, or just send them spam themselves. The main risk here is that the disreputable provider can leverage their knowledge of your connection to the addresses to sell the addresses to one of your business competitors, or even use your brand name in the spam that they send.

This can have a huge reputational effect on your business, along with potential legal consequences. Therefore, make sure you do sufficient research before handing email addresses over to any provider.

Reputable providers of email verification services include, but are not limited to, Email Hippo and Kickbox.

This chapter covered email validation services. They use various methods to tell you the probability that a specific address is valid, and not going to bounce or to be a spam trap. They are useful when addresses are collected offline, before contacting an old list, or when address validation is delayed. Consult the relevant data protection regulations before using these services. The industry has some bad actors, so do due diligence on a provider before trusting them with your list data.

Chapter 7
Bounces and List Hygiene

This chapter covers how to manage bounces and keep your subscriber lists in good condition. It explains how bounces influence deliverability and how they are directly related to the quality of the messages you and sending, or the email addresses you are sending to.

Bounces

A bounce occurs when something goes wrong, and the receiving email server does not accept your message. An email server can bounce a message by either refusing to accept it during the SMTP conversation or sending a *bounce* message back to the sender after acceptance. Bounce messages are sent to the *return-path* address, not the From address. For more information on SMTP and the return-path header, see Chapter 2.

Bounces are either classified as being hard, soft, or block bounces.

Hard bounces

A hard bounce occurs when the bounce message indicates that the address you are trying to reach is unlikely to ever be reachable. This typically occurs when you send to a non-existent address.

If you receive a hard bounce, you should stop sending to that address and remove it from your list. Continuing to deliver messages may damage your sending reputation. For information on sending reputation, see Chapter 8.

Soft Bounces

A soft bounce occurs when the bounce message indicates there is a temporary problem which prevents the message from being delivered on this specific occasion. Soft bounces occur for many reasons, such as the recipient's mailbox being full or the receiving server running out of space.

Another reason for seeing soft bounces is that you are sending messages too quickly and the receiving email server is telling you to "back off and slow down". This can happen when you are warming up a new IP address, as explained in Chapter 8.

Since a soft bounce signifies a temporary failure, you can try to deliver the message to that address again, just not immediately. If you receive three soft bounces in a row over a reasonable length of time, for example two weeks, it is best current practice to treat the soft bounce as you would a hard bounce.

Block Bounces

Block bounces occur when the recipient's email server refuses to accept the message because it either believes it to be spam or thinks that the sending IP has a poor reputation. Blocks can also occur due to the sender's presence on a Realtime Block List (RBL), which are covered in Chapter 5.

To avoid damage to your sending reputation, it is best current practice to pause resending the message until the reason for the block has been addressed.

SMTP status codes

There is no standard format for explaining the reason for a bounce in a bounce message. For example, one bounce reason may be "Disk Full", another may say "No space left on device", and one may just say "Access denied". You must read each bounce message or use specialist *bounce processor* software to understand exactly why bounces are occurring.

Since the SMTP protocol is a standardised way for email servers to talk to each other, it has a standard way of communicating successes and failures. It achieves this by using numeric three-digit status codes. These codes are used during the SMTP conversation in response to each command received by an email server.

Code	**Definition**
2xx	Positive Completion Reply
3xx	Positive Intermediate Reply
4xx	Transient Negative Completion Reply
5xx	Permanent Negative Completion Reply

SMTP status codes are rarely the only information included with a bounce. There is usually a textual description accompanying the code. For example, the bounce message "451 4.3.2 Internal server error" was once used by Yahoo! when temporarily refusing messages.

2xx status codes are part of a normal successful SMTP conversation and should not appear in connection with a bounce.

3xx status codes are also part of a normal SMTP conversation but may show up in a bounce if there is a problem with the configuration of one of the email servers. For example, status code 354 could appear if the sending server stopped the SMTP conversation before transmitting the message.

4xx status codes are often associated with soft bounces as they indicate a temporary problem. For example, status code 450 is often associated with a temporary problem with the recipient's mailbox.

Sometimes, 4xx codes can be related to temporary blocking due to message filtering. For example, Microsoft have used the 451 code in this context:

> *4.7.650 The mail server [x.x.x.x] has been temporarily rate limited due to IP reputation. For e-mail delivery information, see https://postmaster.live.com (S843)[#.prod.protection.outlook.com]*

5xx status codes are often associated with hard bounces as they indicate a permanent problem. For example, status code 550 is often associated with a mailbox not being found, meaning that the address is invalid.

5xx codes are also often associated with blocking due to message filtering. For example, the Barracuda message filter has used code 554 in this context:

> *smtp;554 rejected due to spam URL in content*

Suppression lists

When you use an ESP to send your bulk messages to addresses that bounce, they are added to a suppression list. A suppression list is a segment of your subscriber list which will not be contacted for any reason. Those addresses are *suppressed* by the ESP. The purpose of a suppression list is to prevent a sender from unintentionally damaging their sending reputation by repeatedly sending to addresses which are continuously bouncing. The exact criteria for when an address gets added varies from provider to provider. If you know that a suppressed address is now valid and will not bounce, it is usually possible to manually remove it from the suppression list.

Reducing bounces

To protect your sending reputation, you need to keep your bounce rate consistently low. A bounce rate above two percent should be investigated.

Sending to the occasional invalid email address is a genuine mistake and mail systems are more than happy to let you know that there is a problem with the address through a bounce. However, when you generate many bounces, message filters look at it very differently than a simple mistake. High bounce rates may cause the message filter to start classifying all your messages as spam and this will impact your overall sender reputation.

One reason high volumes of bounces can happen is because you are sending to invalid addresses. This is a classic sign of a spammer or a sender who is buying low quality contact lists.

To maintain a high level of deliverability, bounces need to be kept to a minimum. This can be achieved by not purchasing lists and verifying email addresses prior to bulk sending through a confirmed opt-in process.

Confirmed opt-In

Confirmed Opt-In (COI) is a process of confirming an email address which you have acquired is valid. COI works by sending a confirmation message to the address at the point when you acquire it. If the address is valid, then the recipient will click on the confirmation link embedded in the message. If the address is invalid or the recipient does not confirm, then the address is not added to your list, keeping it clean. This is sometimes referred to as *double opt-in*.

COI is typically used for newsletter subscriptions and when signing up new users to web services. Many ESPs require that you implement confirmed opt-in, and that you can prove to them the date each email address was confirmed. Confirming that recipients have consented to being subscribed to your list is a significant factor in good deliverability.

Address validation

Sometimes confirmed opt-in is simply not possible. This can occur when email addresses are collected off-line, such as during a phone call. Using an email address validation service can reduce the number of potential invalid addresses added to your list in these cases. It is best current practice to apply COI at the earliest opportunity after using a validation service. For more information on validation services, see Chapter 6.

List hygiene

Not sending to invalid email addresses is just one component of managing your subscriber list, known in the industry as practising list hygiene. If there is an issue with your list which hurts deliverability, nothing can be done. Therefore, practising list hygiene is crucial for maintaining strong deliverability. This can be done in several ways:

1. Promptly remove addresses that hard bounce

Addresses that generate bounced email should be removed from your list. Along with keeping your bounce rate low, some mailbox providers identify bad senders as those who repeatedly send to the same invalid email addresses repeatedly.

2. Use confirmed opt-in

If you collect email addresses from online forms, such as with a newsletter subscription, then you should confirm that those email addresses are valid and were not entered by a third party. You can normally enable Confirmed Opt-In through your ESP.

3. Use captcha or nocaptcha on web forms

Automated signups are used by cyber criminals to disable target email addresses by subscription bombing them. This is the process of sending huge volumes of Confirmed Opt-In verification emails to a mailbox for the purposes of overloading and disabling it.

A captcha is designed to protect against automated signups. This is usually achieved by making the user transcribe words displayed in an image or select a common theme from presented images.

Nocaptcha on the other hand works in the background and uses the cookies associated with logins to other platforms along with other means to confirm that you are a real person. Nocaptcha results in less friction for a user during the signup process and will typically fall back to a traditional captcha if it does not work for that user.

If you get dragged into becoming part of a subscription bombing campaign, there is a very high chance that it will cause you or your ESP to be listed on Realtime Block Lists (RBLs) which will impact the deliverability of your email. RBLs are covered in Chapter 5. Many ESPs offer captcha and nocaptcha protection, and web developers can also implement these mechanisms on your website.

4. Honour unsubscribes and removal requests

When a recipient asks you to stop sending them messages, stop immediately. There is no excuse to let a contact linger on a list or in a database once they have told you that they no longer want to hear from you. Newsletter software typically handles this for you automatically, by including an unsubscribe link in every outgoing email.

If you are sending from a Customer Relationship Management (CRM) system which may not include an unsubscribe link, then you need to use a valid and monitored From and Reply-To address so that you can see any removal requests in replies. If you do not remove people when they ask, they are likely to mark your email as spam, which can have consequences for your deliverability beyond their single mailbox. Some mailbox providers even have the capability to monitor a sender's compliance with unsubscribe requests. For more information on how recipient behaviour can affect deliverability, see Chapter 10.

If you use segmentation to divide your large subscriber list, then a single unsubscribe may not work for you. Instead, you can implement a preference centre. A preference centre allows users to pick what segments they wish to subscribe to or unsubscribe from. Many ESPs offer a preference centre capability.

5. Use a *list-unsubscribe* header if possible

The list-unsubscribe header contains information on how to unsubscribe from a mailing list; this is usually an email address, but it can be a link to an online unsubscribe mechanism. While the actual header is not directly visible to the recipient, some mailbox providers and email clients will use this header to create a prominent "unsubscribe" button in your emails.

If the recipient clicks the button, an email is sent to the address in the header and the recipient's address is removed from your contact list.

Many ESPs include the header by default or allow it to be enabled easily. It should be used in addition to the traditional unsubscribe link in a message.

6. Never re-subscribe a former contact

Once a recipient has been removed from a list, do not put them back on that list or another list later, unless they explicitly ask. This is called re-subscribing and will quickly generate complaints and hurt deliverability.

7. Never cross-subscribe a contact

If a contact signs up for one list, you must never silently subscribe them to other lists you operate, regardless of how relevant you think those lists might be to them. When it comes to list subscriptions, there is no such thing as implied permission; a contact must explicitly request to be added to a list. This practice is known as cross-subscribing and, like re-subscribing, can quickly generate complaints and affect your deliverability.

8. Deal with customer complaints

Customers can actively complain in two ways about messages which they have received: by reporting it as spam in their email client or webmail, or by contacting you directly. When they mark a message as spam, that information is often transmitted to your ESP who will show it on your dashboard. If you know the address that generated the complaint, immediately remove it from your contact list. When you are contacted directly, always acknowledge the complaint, and confirm that you have removed their address. Do not just silently remove the address because the contact will have no way of knowing this, and they may report the mail as spam anyway. If your email activities generate too many complaints, you will start to be blocked and filtered automatically into spam folders.

This chapter covered how to handle bounced emails and keep your contact list in good order. You should monitor bounces, as they can indicate problems with invalid addresses and filtering. Message filters have a low threshold for bulk sending to invalid addresses and will mark your mail spam if you generate too many bounces. Invalid addresses need to be removed promptly from a contact list. Sending a confirmation message when you first receive a new address is called confirmed opt-in and is considered best practice. To keep a contact list in good order, use confirmed opt-in, protect forms with a captcha or nocaptcha, remove people that do not want to be contacted, never subscribe people to lists without their knowledge, and deal with complaints promptly and properly.

Chapter 8
Domain and IP reputation

This chapter explains the importance of maintaining a good sender reputation for email deliverability. It covers how both domain and IP address-based reputation systems work. Each message filter will calculate reputation differently. It is possible to have a great reputation with one mailbox provider while a poor one with another. This chapter takes a general approach to discussing reputation filtering and does not focus on any one provider implementation.

Every domain, sub-domain, IP address, and even IP network, has a reputation associated with it. The reputation of a sender is based on the quality of the messages they send over time. Depending on the individual message filter, the time can be anything from a few hours to a few weeks, even as much as a few months. The important thing to understand is that a poor sending reputation of any kind can take time to shake and may result in deliverability issues. The best approach is to understand what can affect your reputation before you start sending, so that you begin to build a positive reputation from day one.

Domain Reputation

The domain names you use in messages, especially the domain used in the From field is often inspected by reputation-based systems for signs that they could be associated with spamming or malicious behaviour.

In general, sub-domains (for example, email.example.com) have an independent reputation to the base domain. However, if the base domain already has a very poor reputation, new sub-domains created off it may inherit some or all that reputation.

While domain reputation is largely based on what the domain is used for, you can take steps to reduce the chances of filter false positives by ensuring that it looks legitimate.

1. Watch the registration date

When you register a new domain name, the creation date is recorded and can be publicly queried. Spammers like to register lots of domain names, then throw them away when they get blocked. This has not gone unnoticed by operators of filters. Therefore, ideally you should wait until a domain name is at least six months old before sending bulk messages.

2. Keep accurate domain contract details

When you register a new domain, you provide contact details. These details, like the creation and expiration dates, can sometimes be publicly queried. Some filter and spam trap operators will query this information while investigating a domain. Historically, this contact information was often abused by spammers to harvest email addresses. As a result of this, domain registrars began to offer paid services which mask the contact details. Privacy focused regulations, such as the GDPR in Europe, also caused this information to be withheld.

If you have the option, avoid concealing the registration contact details of a domain and ensure that they are accurate.

3. Be careful using trendy Top-Level Domains (TLDs)

In recent years over one thousand new general Top-Level Domains (TLDs) have been made available for registration. They have catchy names such as .blog, .online, and .science. About 30 million of these have been registered and they are now appearing in the mainstream. While it might seem like an appealing idea to use one of these for sending email, be careful as it may impact your deliverability with some smaller mailbox providers.

Why? To stimulate growth, one-year registrations of many of these TLDs, such as XYZ, are given away by domain registrars for free or for a nominal fee. This results in them being resold and used by spammers. Additionally, the major blocklist provider Spamhaus publishes a list of the TLDs they most frequently see being used in spam messages. Consequently, smaller mailbox providers with unsophisticated message filters may arbitrarily penalise senders using some of these new TLDs.

4. Check the history of a domain

Before buying a used vehicle, wise buyers ask a mechanic to check it over. You need to do the same with domain names. Ideally before you buy a domain name, and certainly before you start sending email using a new domain, you should check to see if it was previously associated with a poor reputation. You can do this by using the tools outlined later in this chapter.

Sometimes, unused domains can be covertly abused by spammers. So, even if you are not buying a domain name and simply using one which you already owned but never used before, you should check its reputation.

5. Use a reputable DNS provider

An organisation's whole ability to send (and receive) email relies on the Domain Name Service (DNS) (see Chapter 2). Email authentication (see Chapter 11) also depends on DNS to work.

When a domain name is connected to a poor-quality DNS service, it can affect deliverability. This is because the service is not fast enough in answering the queries from the receiving email systems. This can result in email authentication failing, along with the providers marking the domain name as not being properly set up. This causes a massive hit to your deliverability and may even contribute to your domain name being flagged as having a poor reputation.

Normally you do not need to worry about the reliability of your DNS provider. If you are using the DNS service provided by your domain registrar or using a paid commercial DNS service, you should have no problems. Issues typically occur when you use the DNS provided by a cheap web hosting provider, or you try to host it on your own servers, without having the needed experience.

6. Accept mail to the abuse@ address

If you send email of any kind, but especially bulk email, then there is a convention that you create an abuse@ mailbox (for example, abuse@example.com) where people can report perceived spam from your domain. It is strongly advisable to create and monitor such a mailbox as this is often the first place you will see warning signs about your deliverability. If someone believes that a message you sent is spam, just remove them from your list, let them know, and move on. Never debate or argue with anyone who has taken the time to complain directly to you, instead of to your Email Service Provider (ESP) or their own mailbox provider. This mailbox will also receive automated alerts about your sending behaviour. Many of these alerts will be useless, but some may be relevant.

IP Reputation

No matter how you send email, via an ESP, or your own email server, the recipient's mailbox provider will see it originating from one or more IP addresses. Like domain names, those IP addresses will have a reputation associated with them.

IP reputation is an overall score or weighting that a message filter assigns to an IP address. Reputation can be based on multiple data points, such as listings on prominent blocklists, spam trap hits, the reputation of surrounding IPs, the reputation of websites that are linked to in messages, and how recipients interact with messages. IP reputation is usually calculated over time, such as sampling of the mail flow over a month or more of activity. Not every message filter calculates sender reputation, but those that do all have their own unique criteria.

Messages can either be sent from a shared or a dedicated IP address. Shared IPs, sometimes referred to as "shared pools", allow multiple senders to use the same IP or set of IPs. Mailbox providers nearly always use shared IPs, and many ESPs offer them as an option to their clients. The opposite of shared IPs are dedicated IPs. Dedicated IPs are where one or more IP addresses are assigned exclusively to a single sender.

Shared IP reputation

Shared IPs have a collective reputation based on the overall assessment of the mail originating from that pool. This is not an issue if all the senders are following best practices and sending approximately the same volume of messages. The reputation of shared IPs suffers when either most senders fail to follow best practices, or a single bad sender is responsible for a disproportionate volume of messages. Shared IP reputation is also susceptible to a single sender getting hacked and starting to relay spam, even for a short period of time.

Dedicated IP reputation

The reputation of a dedicated IP is typically based on the current sender and their mail flow. That means that when you are assigned a new dedicated IP, it does not normally inherit the reputation of the former user. Reputable ESPs will allow IPs assigned to former clients to "cool down" before assigning them to a new one. This minimises the risk of any residual reputation created by the previous sender influencing the new one. There are occasions where the reputation of a dedicated IP is influenced by the reputations of surrounding IPs. This is known as *reputational proximity.*

Reputational Proximity

IP addresses do not exist in a vacuum. They are surrounded on each side by other IP addresses in the same range. For example, the IP address 192.168.1.40 has both 192.168.1.39 and 192.168.1.41 as direct neighbours. The collective reputations of neighbouring IPs can sometimes influence the reputation of a single IP located in the same neighbourhood, even if it has never been used to send messages.

That collective reputation may be good or bad. If a message filter decides that the collective reputation of an IP range is poor, it can make it hard for an individual sender to build their own distinctive reputation on a single IP in that range. Ideally, you should not be sending from bad neighbourhoods as you will continually encounter issues created by those bad senders in your proximity. Reputable ESPs do not have spammers as customers. They also segregate their IP space based on customer reputation, meaning that customers of similar reputation are kept together.

When to choose a dedicated IP

For general one-to-one email, the shared pools that mailbox providers use are best. For bulk email, using dedicated IPs is normally better as you have more control over the reputation. However, there are some cases where shared IPs may be better. Filters need a statistically significant number of messages to learn from and calculate IP reputation. This means that they favour higher volumes and consistent sending patterns. Relying on the collective reputation of a shared IP pool is better for infrequent senders and those sending below one thousand messages per month.

A dedicated IP needs to be sending at least one thousand messages every month to have any chance at building and maintaining a reputation. Ideally the IP should send at least five hundred thousand messages per month for optimal results. One reason why higher volumes are better is because this often gives senders more options in case of a problem with their IP reputation. High volume senders often have more sophisticated mailing programmes which allow them to identify and suppress the campaign that caused a reputation problem.

It is also not uncommon for a sender to begin on a shared pool and then graduate to a dedicated IP when their volumes grow to the point where it may overwhelm the shared pool.

How many IPs?

How many dedicated IP addresses you will need depends on two factors: the volume of messages you are sending and the distribution of mailbox providers on your contact list. A single dedicated IP address is usually good for sending about 30 - 40 million emails per month or about one million emails a day. The distribution of mailbox providers is important because you do not want to send close to that volume of emails to any single mailbox provider from a single IP address. It is best practice to spread each IP's sending over a reasonably even distribution of providers. Otherwise, the receiving mailbox provider will see a huge volume of email from one single IP and their filters may mistake you for being a spammer.

For example, if you know that eighty percent of your contacts use Yahoo! addresses, then you might split the sending over more than one IP address to make sure that Yahoo! did not get hit with a disproportionate number of messages from a single IP address compared to other addresses. Your ESP will advise you on how many IP addresses you need based on their own policies and infrastructure capabilities.

Warming an IP

New dedicated IP addresses often need to be "warmed". This is the process of gradually introducing messages from the IP to the filters. This gives the message filters time to get used to the quality of the mail flow and begin assigning a reputation.

When you neglect to warm an IP address, message filters may start to throttle or block the IP because receiving such a sudden high volume of messages from a previously unknown IP is a common spammer tactic. Spammers sometimes try to flood mailbox providers with messages, hoping that enough messages would reach inboxes before complaints would cause the filters to start blocking.

Once an IP is warmed to a target volume, incremental growth, such as through new sign-ups or increased newsletter frequency, does not require further warming. However, you may also need to warm up an existing dedicated IP if you intend to suddenly increase the monthly volume by a significant amount. For example, if you intend to double the volume from three to six million messages per month. Dramatically changing the composition of the mail flow may also require a new warm up. For example, changing the From domain and sending to entirely new recipients.

Warm-up plans

A warm-up plan tells a sender the maximum number of messages that they should send on a weekly basis. Each week, that maximum number increases until the target volume is reached. The target volume is the total monthly number of messages which are intended to be sent from the IP or IPs on a regular basis.

A warm-up plan may look something like this:

Week	Maximum messages per-send
Week 1	130,000
Week 2	170,000
Week 3	230,000
Week 4	310,000
Week 5	420,000
Week 6	560,000
Week 7	750,000
Week 8	1,000,000

In this example, the sender would be careful not to send more than 130,000 messages for any scheduled send during the first week, 170,000 for the second and so on until the target volume of 1,000,000 was reached.

To successfully warm up a marketing stream, you will need both engaged recipients and fresh content. At least one mailbox provider deliberately places some messages into the spam folder during a warming to see if the recipients take them out. If your content is stale and recipients are not expecting your messages, getting them to proactively remove messages from the spam folder can be challenging.

Transactional messages are often triggered in real-time by user events. That type of mail flow cannot be used to warm an IP in the same way as scheduled sends from marketing flows. Luckily, you may not need to warm a new IP for a transactional mail flow. The more sophisticated message filters used by large mailbox providers can distinguish between marketing and transactional messages. These providers do not want to upset their users by having "password reset" type messages delayed or placed in spam. Therefore, they rarely throttle or block a new transactional feed on a dedicated IP. However, if you are planning to send more than ten thousand transactional messages per day on new dedicated IPs, then you may benefit from a special type of IP warming which your provider should be able to automatically control.

ESPs will typically either create a bespoke warming plan for your sending pattern or provide guidance on how to create your own.

Maintaining domain and IP reputation

Once you have successfully started using a domain or completed a warm-up plan, you need to take certain steps to ensure that sending reputation is maintained.

1. Avoid spikes in sending

Reputational systems use statistical models to identify unusual volume patterns, so avoid any sudden increase in the sending volume or frequency of your email. If for some reason you need to dramatically increase the volume or frequency coming from an IP address, then you will need a new warm-up plan to gradually move towards the new rates.

If you are acquiring new subscribers on a regular basis, such as with a newsletter, then that type of growth is not considered a spike as it is broadly predictable.

2. Keep an eye on bounces and spam complaints

A sudden increase in either bounces or spam complaints means that there is a problem with your list which will potentially cause problems with reputation. It is often advisable to stop sending until you solve the issue and then gradually start sending again. Do not ignore bounces or spam complaints, always deal with them, and try to identify the root causes.

3. **Monitor sending reputation**

There are many services which can provide information on domain and IP reputation. Microsoft's Smart Network Data Services (SNDS) allows senders to see their IP reputation on their consumer (Outlook.com) mailbox filters. Google Postmaster Tools (GPT) will allow you to view multiple reputation metrics for both the domain and the associated sending IPs. There are also third-party services offered by companies such as Cisco and IBM. These services can provide different results for the same domain or IP. This is normal and caused by their information being based on what their message filters or sensor networks detect.

4. **Sign your messages with DKIM**

Regardless of domains or IPs, one very important way that a sender can distinguish themselves and build and help independent reputation is to DKIM sign their messages. For more information on DKIM signing, see Chapter 11.

IP certification services

Certification (or accreditation) services offer senders a method of having their IPs certified as sources of high-quality messages. They typically require the sender to go through a formal process which can include proving that the IP has not sent spam over a certain period or enabling strict email authentication. Each provider has their own criteria.

Certification services are used by some mailbox providers to allow senders to be treated more leniently when it comes to filtering. Senders can lose certification if they fail to keep to the agreed criteria.

Being a certified sender is not required for email deliverability, even when sending bulk emails. Most large mailbox providers require senders do nothing other than not send spam and keep their bounces and complaints to a minimum. So, while it is certainly true that these services may not be as crucial as they were in the past, there are still some very valid reasons for considering their use.

Improved delivery to particular providers

If you are encountering problems delivering bulk email to a particular mailbox provider, then you may benefit from exploring if they look favourably on accreditation from a particular provider.

Additional sender benefits

Some mailbox providers may provide certified senders with additional benefits over regular senders. For example, a certified sender might have the images in their emails automatically load in a provider's webmail facility, while this is not allowed for regular senders.

Helps compliance with best practices

Certification programs are typically based around best practices, such as those explained in this book. Large organisations with sending capability spread across several business units often benefit from the discipline that a certification programme provides.

When considering if you should use certification service, it is crucial to find out exactly which mailbox providers are signed up to use them, as coverage can vary greatly. You can normally find this out by asking the vendor directly. You must make sure that their coverage matches a significant portion of the providers that supply mailbox services to your subscribers.

This chapter covered the importance of domain and IP address reputation on deliverability. Domain names need to look like they have not been registered by spammers. This is mainly achieved by making sure you do not send bulk messages from domains registered in the previous six months and being careful about using fancy TLDs. Sub-domains can have their own independent sending reputations. Sending from shared IPs means that your reputation is often only as good as the least bad sender on the pool. Dedicated IPs allow you more control over your reputation. A warming plan is used to build the sending reputation of new dedicated IP addresses. DKIM signing messages can help with building reputation. Certification services allow you to get special treatment with the providers that use them. These services are not as popular as they once were and have limited coverage with mailbox providers.

Chapter 9
Content Filtering

This chapter covers content filters. These are filters which work on the content (or body) of email messages looking for potential security risks and spam. They are both widely used and widely misunderstood. While content filtering is not intended to interfere with legitimate senders, mistakes can occur. This chapter explains the main types of content filter and how legitimate senders can avoid being accidentally caught by them.

Lexical analysis

Historically, scanning the text of an email was how most spam was identified. In the early days, filtering was based on keywords known to be associated with spam. Over time, those keywords were replaced by pattern-matching algorithms and machine learning. Scanning for security threats such as phishing are also now a component of these types of filters.

Modern lexical (text) analysis is very advanced and legitimate senders no longer need to worry about including a "banned" keyword or phrase such as "free offer" in their messages. When a legitimate sender encounters a problem with a text filter, it is usually because the email has an unintentional similarity to a common phishing or security threat.

The one exception to single words or phrases causing problems with these filters is when they are deployed by individual organisations, often referred to as "B2B filters". In these cases, it is very possible that the presence of a particular word or phrase may cause a message to be quarantined or even bounced. For example, an organisation might filter messages with the phrase "click here to view your order" as a way of stopping a particular malicious message. However, months later, that filter could block a legitimate message from a new supplier.

Luckily it is not too difficult to make sure that legitimate messages do not look suspicious.

Use your own domain
Domain names have reputations associated with them (see Chapter 8). Some content filters associate negative reputations to the domains that appear in messages which they flag as spam, or a security risk.

When you include links in your message with shared domains, such as a link-shortener or an ESP click-tracking link, you run the risk of that shared domain having a poor reputation because it was previously associated with filtered messages.

Therefore, where possible, always use a domain which you control for any links in the message. Most link-shortener services, file sharing platforms, and ESPs provide an option to use your own domain instead of their shared domain.

Be careful with redirects
Single redirects in a message, for example, a click-tracking link that then re-directs to the destination website, are typically not a problem. What can cause problems are links with multiple redirects before the destination. This is a technique often used by spammers to conceal the true destination. Some filters will not look favourable on messages with these types of complex redirects, so it is best to avoid using them.

Avoid linking to dynamic content
Many filters will follow the links in messages to see if they lead to sites that may be a risk to users, such as those hosting malware. Some websites serve dynamic content based on the detected web-browser or IP address of visitors. While there are legitimate reasons to do this, it may look suspicious to some filters. This is mainly because the link scanner software that filters use is often detected as a web browser with limited functionality; in response, the site serves it content different to everyone else. When this happens, the filter may believe that the site is suspicious.

Pay attention linking to remote content
A common method used to bypass virus filters is to store the virus on an external service, such as Dropbox or Google Drive and link to it from the email. For this reason, try to avoid externally hosted content. If you are unable to attach files or embed images in the message and must host

them externally, always make sure they are hosted on the same single domain name from which you sent the email.

These are the main causes for legitimate email being filtered, but it is not a definitive list. Investigation and testing are often required to identify exactly why email is being caught by text analysis filtering.

URL Blocklists

RBLs (see Chapter 5) list IP addresses, IP networks, and domain names, which are associated with spam. URL blocklists, on the other hand, contain actual web site addresses. After email has been received all the links included are scanned for their presence on a URL blocklist. A web address can appear on a blocklist for several reasons. Typically, it is either because the site is being promoted in spam messages, or because the site is hosting a virus or malware which is being promoted in spam messages.

Legitimate senders are normally added to these blocklists because they get hacked and their web server is used to host viruses. Like RBLs, each URL blocklist will have its own delisting process, detailed on the operator's website.

Checksum Based Filtering

Checksum filtering is based on the principle that spam emails may look alike, but they are not identical. When an email is reported as spam to a checksum system, it creates a "fuzzy" checksum of the email. A checksum is a small digital signature of data, in this case an email message. The checksum can be used to verify that the email is identical to the one from which the checksum was originally created. A fuzzy checksum leaves out some aspects of the original message, so it will match emails that look very similar, but not identical, to the original. When an email server uses a checksum-based filter, it creates a checksum for every incoming email and compares it to known fuzzy checksums of spam emails.

Checksum systems often have internet-based databases. This allows many email servers to query the database and identify spam emails. Legitimate senders normally do not have to worry about their emails getting caught up in checksum-based filters, because recipients are not reporting their emails as spam. When it does happen, it is usually the result of a sender copying the same publicly available HTML email template that a spammer is using. It can also be caused by a security breach which resulted in spam being sent out through an email account belonging to the sending organisation. Commercial checksum filter operators provide a delisting service in such cases.

Checksum filters which are operated on a non-commercial basis often do not provide any formal delisting process. Instead, delisting occurs when enough of the system's users mark the incorrectly flagged email as not being spam. In practice, such delisting systems rarely work as intended. It is sometimes possible for a legitimate sender to get around a checksum filter by making changes to the body and signature of their email. This is because the match is commonly caused either by chunks of copied HTML formatting which were also used by a spammer or, in the case of a hacking incident, the email signature which was sent out with the spam being relayed. Having your signature trigger a checksum filter is a worst-case scenario, because rebranding may be the only course of action.

Brand-name based filtering

Some mailbox providers have special filters which specifically look for the use of major brand names in messages and check whether they are being sent from or linked to the brand's regular domain name. The purpose of these filters is to identify attempted fraud within a specific set of brands which are commonly impersonated by spammers. This could be, for example, an email promoting a prominent credit card provider but being sent from a third-party address and linking to a completely unrelated domain. If you are a large brand or you are engaged to promote one, try to send the emails from the brand's main domain, or use a subdomain off the main domain. Also, try and keep any links in the email going straight to the brand's domain.

Content checking tools

There are many tools, offered as both standalone services and built into ESP platforms which claim to check your messages for the likelihood that they will be flagged as spam by a content filter. They often attribute a score to the tested message and provide a list of potential problems. The recommendations are typically about image to text ratios, the density between the font colours, and the presence of links on blocklists.

It is important to understand that most of these tools are all based on the same underlying open-source content scanner called SpamAssassin. SpamAssassin has been around since the early 2000s and is still being updated today. Today, this software is not used by large mailbox providers. It may still be used by some smaller providers and some commercial email scanning solutions.

While following the recommendations from such tools will not hurt the chances of a message reaching the inbox, bear in mind that they do not reflect how modern content filters classify messages.

This chapter covered the popular types of content-based filtering. Text analysis is the oldest. These days it is very advanced and no longer based on single "keywords". There are some steps legitimate senders can take to avoid their emails being mistakenly caught by content filtering. URL blocklists work like RBLs but are based on the actual links in a message. Sites that are advertised in spam or links to viruses are listed. Checksum filters use digital signatures to match new emails with previously identified spam messages. Legitimate senders normally get caught up in URL blocklists and checksum-based filters because of security breaches. It is possible to get delisted from a URL blacklist. Only commercially operated checksum filters provide a guaranteed method of removal. Major brands should send from and link to their own domains. Using content checker tools will not do any harm, but they do not reflect how modern filters work.

Chapter 10
Engagement Filters

This chapter explains how engagement-based filtering works, how it can affect deliverability, and how to address it.

Engagement filters use machine learning and advanced analytics to monitor how recipients interact with your messages, to determine whether future messages should be classified as spam. They work in real time after messages have successfully arrived in an inbox and are based solely on how recipients feel about your email. They are used by large mailbox providers and some corporate mail filters, in addition to other types of filtering. Engagement filters typically only apply to bulk email and not one-to-one personal emails.

Key behaviours

Every implementation of behavioural filtering is slightly different, but in general you want recipients to practise the following positive behaviours

- Read the email
- Add the sender to the address book
- Forward or reply to the message
- Mark the email as "not spam" or remove it from the spam folder

On the other hand, you want your recipients to avoid the following negative behaviours

- Report the email as spam
- Delete the email without opening it
- Block the sender
- Open the email and delete immediately

Engagement filtering works on aggregated data from many recipients and no single recipient can influence your reputation. So, you do not need to worry about somebody accidentally deleting or marking your message as spam.

Mailbox providers known to incorporate engagement filtering into their reputation calculations include Google, Yahoo!, and Microsoft.

Identifying engagement-based filtering

To identify if your email is being classified as spam by engagement filtering, you first need to rule out any other type of filtering that is being applied. Engagement blocks are typically based on bulk emails (not one-to- one emails) so you should be able to send a message to a test account and contact a few subscribers individually. Once you are reasonably confident that your email is not being subjected to any other type of filtering, look for unusual patterns with individual mailbox providers such as very low open or engagement rates compared to other providers. Inbox placement monitoring tools can also help you identify engagement filtering, and these are explained in Chapter 4.

Recovering from engagement-based blocking

If your email is classified as spam because of engagement filtering, you must first understand why, before trying to recover.

Problems with engagement typically relate to anger at receiving an unsolicited message, apathy, where the recipients perceive no value in your content, or a content/audience mismatch.

Addressing these issues falls outside of the remit of this book and is usually a job for marketing and communications professionals.

Even if you are subjected to engagement filtering, it is usually possible to get very low volumes of your marketing emails delivered into subscriber inboxes. This is because low volumes of email are typically treated differently from bulk mails. You can use this to your advantage as part of the remedial process by reaching out to small numbers of subscribers directly to measure responses. Be careful if your marketing colleagues use A/B (split) testing that you keep the frequency and volume very low, preferably in the double digits, otherwise the filters might kick in.

Looking at your historical sending metrics for that affected mailbox provider can often point you in the direction of the campaign or segment that triggered the filtering. If you are sending unsolicited messages, the engagement filtering is likely working as expected.

Once you believe that you have addressed the cause of the issue, you can either try and encourage positive behaviours by trickling emails out to your list or contacting the affected subscribers by other means to alert them in advance to look out for your email in the spam folder. Having a non-email-based method of reaching list subscribers, such as through social media platforms, can be very useful in these instances. Removing emails from the spam folder, opening, and reading the emails, along with adding the sender to their address book are excellent positive behaviours which you should encourage amongst your subscribers.

Another option is to take advantage of the fact that the filters work on aggregated results from samples of received emails. That means that if you can spread engaged subscribers evenly throughout your delivery cycle, the filters will constantly see positive behaviours in any sample of your email that they analyse. This only works if your content is genuinely engaging, and you have a sufficient volume of engaged users. Getting around a behavioural block is often a complicated timely process which involves a lot of trial and error.

Avoidance

There are several strategies which you can employ to stay on the right side of behavioural filters from the outset. This is advisable because of the often-significant effort to overcome one of these filters.

Send relevant and engaging content

This is the number one way to avoid having problems with behavioural filters. Recipients will naturally open and read content that is consistently interesting and engaging to them.

Do not be afraid of interacting with subscribers

It is in your best interest for subscribers to reply to your emails, so avoid using unmonitored or inactive From addresses, for example do-not-reply@example.com. Encourage subscribers to reply to emails as one of your communications channels.

Make sure the subscribers ask for your emails

Sending emails to subscribers who did not ask for them is a sure way to generate negative responses. For bulk marketing emails, this means implementing double opt-in and practising good list hygiene as explained in Chapter 7. For transactional emails, this means not enabling every possible notification by default and clearly communicating at sign-up which ones are enabled.

Remove unengaged addresses

Periodically removing addresses that do not engage in any way with your emails will decrease the number of negative behavioural indicators. You can often achieve this by running targeted list re-confirmation campaigns. This is a controversial strategy because of the potential to remove future customers or those that use privacy tools to obscure their message interactions. Your overall level of list engagement will determine if you need to employ this strategy.

Encourage subscribers to add you to their address book

Being added to a subscriber's address book is a very positive behavioural indicator and often comes with other benefits, such as images being loaded automatically. You should actively encourage this practice, even going as far as providing how-to instructions for common mailbox providers.

Develop a secondary channel

Plan for the worst and have at least a second channel to reach your subscribers just in case. Having a non-email way to reach a statistically significant portion of your subscriber list allows you to still reach them with a "take our next email out of spam" type of message.

Be wary of "fake engagement" services

In the past few years, several commercial services have appeared which claim to improve a sender's standing with engagement filters, normally those used by Google. These services operate by trying to cheat the engagement filter though using fake engagement signals. These services are not intended for legitimate senders, but for those types of senders who are unable to create positive engagement organically. The services work by relaying automatically generated messages from the user through Gmail to other email accounts which they also control. These recipient accounts then automatically "engage" with the messages and reply to them. None of this is following Google's terms and conditions and could go the same way as panel data services did (see Chapter 4) any day. If you are a legitimate sender, you do not need these services.

This chapter covered engagement filtering, which uses how recipients engage with bulk emails as a way of identifying potential spam. Positive behaviours work in your favour while negative ones will work against you. Sending content your recipients want along with encouraging positive behaviours is the best way to stay on the good side of these types of filters. Having a secondary channel to reach subscribers is good future proofing just in case you trigger an engagement-based filter. Avoid "fake engagement" tools.

Chapter 11
Email Authentication

This chapter covers how email authentication can influence deliverability. The three core authentication protocols are covered, along with one adjacent protocol which has become a near-universal requirement. An emerging protocol which is dependent on the three core protocols is also briefly covered. There is a lot more to authentication than improving deliverability, however in keeping with the purpose of this book, this chapter only focuses on the deliverability aspects of email authentication.

Overview

Email authentication is the name given to a family of complementary protocols used to prove to a mailbox provider that a sender is who they say they are. These protocols were developed to combat fraud and sender impersonation by cyber criminals. Over time, certain aspects of email authentication have become essential for email deliverability, especially when sending large volumes of messages.

All three email authentication protocols are based on the Domain Name System (DNS) which, if improperly modified, can temporarily break your email, or even knock your domain name off the Internet. So, an understanding of DNS is strongly advised before implementing any authentication. For more information on DNS, see Chapter 2.

Forward-confirmed reverse DNS

Forward-confirmed reverse DNS (FCrDNS) is a method used to check if a sending email server is trying to spoof its hostname. In the early days of internet email, receiving email servers often based filtering decisions on the hostname of a sending server, so ensuring that it was not spoofed was a concern. These days FCrDNS has pretty much become a universal requirement for delivering any volume of messages.

To understand how FCrDNS works, you first need to understand "reverse DNS". Normally when people talk about DNS, they are referring to "forward DNS", which relates to resources associated with domain names. For example, the MX records which list the email servers responsible for incoming messages for the domain. For more information on MX records, see chapter 2.

However, resources can also be associated with IP addresses. This is commonly referred to as "reverse DNS". Reverse DNS is managed by the owner of the IP address, typically a data centre or Internet Service Provider (ISP). In forward DNS, an A *(address)* record associates an IP address with a hostname. In reverse DNS, a PTR *(pointer)* record associates a hostname with an IP address. It is the IP address owner who controls creating or modifying a PTR record.

FCrDNS means that the forward DNS lookup of an email server's hostname matches the reverse DNS lookup. This is a useful test because it requires that a sender has access to the reverse DNS for their IP, something which people spoofing a hostname cannot achieve.

ESPs manage FCrDNS settings on behalf of the clients. The only time a sender may need to think about reverse DNS is if they are setting up their own internet-hosted email server.

Sender Policy Framework

Sender Policy Framework (SPF) is an email authentication protocol that is used to identify which message sources (email servers) are authorised to send messages on behalf of a domain. Like FCrDNS, SPF also works on the IP address of the sending server. However, SPF allows a sender to provide a list of authorised IP addresses. This is useful, since today many senders use multiple providers to send messages on their behalf. SPF stores its information in the SPF Record.

The SPF Record

The SPF record is a DNS TXT record that is stored in the domain used in the address communicated in the "MAIL FROM" command during the SMTP conversation. This domain is also the one contained in the return-path message header. For more information on SMTP commands and message headers, see Chapter 2. Receiving email servers compare the IP of incoming email server against the list in the SPF record.

In the following example of an SPF record, a single IP is explicitly allowed, along with whatever IP the hostname *email.example.com* resolves to at the time the SPF check is performed.

```
v=spf1 +ip4:192.168.1.1 +a:email.example.com ~all
```

If the IP of the sending server does not match any of those listed, then the SPF default policy is applied.

SPF default policy

Every SPF record has a default policy. This policy recommends how a receiver handles messages that come from sources not listed in the SPF record. The default policy is typically either to indicate that email is explicitly forbidden ("-all"), or that the email is not explicitly permitted from the source ("~all"). Do not concern yourself with the nuanced differences between these two policies. From a deliverability perspective, it is only important to ensure that any server delivering email on behalf of the sending domain is covered, so that the default policy is never reached and applied. However, in practice, many providers only treat the default policy as a signal for the message filters and do not reject messages that fail SPF tests.

Including third party SPF records

When relaying messages through a third party, such as your mailbox provider, you are sometimes asked to modify the SPF record on your sending domain. This is because these providers control their own SPF record and will provide you with the information needed to have their SPF record referenced in your SPF record. This removes the need for you to worry about the third party changing the names or IP addresses of their email servers.

You must add new message sources to the existing SPF record, and always in between the version ("v=spf1") at the beginning, and the default policy (e.g., "~all") at the very end.

For example, when you use Google as a mailbox provider, they ask you to add "include:_spf.google.com" to the SPF record of your domain.

```
v=spf1 +a:email.example.com +include:_spf.google.com ~all
```

DNS lookup limit

The SPF protocol was designed in simpler times, when senders did not outsource a lot of their sending to third parties. There was also a concern that the DNS would be "overloaded" with queries from this new protocol and create delivery delays though SPF checks. Therefore, a limit of ten DNS lookups is built into the protocol. This means that any time a hostname is encountered, for example, "+a:mail.example.com", it counts as one lookup. If the lookup count exceeds ten, then a receiver is permitted to consider the whole SPF record invalid and abandon the SPF check. Sometimes this lookup limit can cause SPF tests to fail and result in deliverability issues. However, many mailbox providers either completely ignore the limit, or extend it to something sensible for modern sending behaviours. "Flattening" the SPF record is another way to avoid the lookup limit. Flattening involves converting every entry that needs a DNS lookup into either a "ip4:" or "ip6:" entry. These entries are direct IPv4 or IPv6 IP addresses or ranges and do not require DNS lookups.

Common mistakes

There are two common mistakes made with SPF. The first is to delete the existing SPF record when making changes. This is often due to a lack of understanding of how SPF works, along with a "cut and paste" from a vendor knowledge base. The second is to add an entirely new second SPF record, instead of amending the existing one. Both mistakes will break your email authentication and impact on deliverability, since an invalid or duplicate SPF record is the same as having none.

DomainKeys Identified Mail

DomainKeys Identified Mail (DKIM) is an email authentication protocol which uses cryptographic signatures to allow an email message to be verifiably associated with a domain name. DKIM has many applications. DKIM helps deliverability by allowing message filters to easily identify mail flows belonging to specific senders, which helps build sending reputation.

How it works

The sender, through their MTA or provider, creates a pair of encryption keys, one public and one private. The private key can cryptographically sign information that only the corresponding public key can decrypt and verify. The public key is published as a TXT record in the DNS and the private key is stored on the MTA or by the provider.

DKIM does not encrypt the message. Instead, it creates cryptographic hashes of certain message headers and the body of the message. It is these hashes which are verified against the actual data in the received message. This information is contained in the DKIM-Signature message header.

The DKIM-Signature header

Messages signed by DKIM have a special DKIM-Signature message header. This header contains information on the location of the public key, the cryptographic hashes, and technical information about the signature process.

```
DKIM-Signature: v=1; a=rsa-sha256;
c=relaxed/relaxed; d=example.com; s=default;
t=1459868954;
bh=U7SL0ftoHW0qZuimyQ2EjpuLTjMa4fIPWK0bYzFsY3o=;
h=Subject:From:From:Subject;
b=GzncbPNyJqjmXnv746KYvmUbEr59hmzuJeybvZcwjNbEDnmo
kMlSFVfKTBiNC6uV9lskpw5ZdGf8YcuJnjxLy/nh08dKrbCkNz
QJ1q6p9zMboE/kCimIPIrcFbAatlzVEAH+ghD/cXma9eHEsT7A
p3vugvAB9uQ2QwWczJWRIWo=
```

Messages can be signed by multiple DKIM keys. meaning that they will have more than one DKIM-Signature header. This is common when sending through an ESP as the ESP will often sign the message themselves for various reasons, including being able to receive complaints via Feedback Loops (FBLs). For more information on FBLs, see Chapter 3.

For deliverability, the important piece of information in the header is the signing domain. This is the domain where the DKIM public key is stored. The signing domain is the domain after the "d=" in the message header. In the above example, the signing domain is "example.com". Knowing the signing domain is important, as you can check to see if the DKIM is "aligned".

DKIM alignment

When you DKIM sign with the same domain that is used in the From field, it is referred to as DKIM alignment. DKIM alignment is important for deliverability. While you can DKIM sign a message with any domain, alignment shows that you control the domain used in the From field. Having access to the DNS for the domain to add the public key is considered evidence of control. This control can send a positive signal to many message filters and helps them identify your mail streams. If you have the option to align your DKIM, you should take it. DKIM alignment is supported by the majority of ESP and CRM solutions. It is often referred to as "white label" or "custom" DKIM. When you align your DKIM you will need to add a CNAME or TXT record to the DNS of the signing domain.

Common problems

There are many factors which can cause DKIM to fail. Anti-virus software can modify the message by adding a "scanned by" type signature. Modifying the message will cause the DKIM to fail. Incorrectly adding the public key to the DNS will prevent the receiver from verifying the DKIM signature, causing DKIM to fail. Other problems relate to the specifics of how DKIM is deployed and are outside of the scope of this book.

DMARC

Domain-based Message Authentication, Reporting, and Conformance (DMARC) is an email authentication protocol which attempts to prevent unauthorised use of a domain name in the From field of a message. It works by applying a policy layer on top of the existing SPF and DKIM authentication applied to messages.

DMARC requires that either SPF or DKIM be aligned and successfully pass. SPF alignment means that the return-path domain matches the domain in the From field. DKIM alignment is explained in the previous section. DMARC applies a policy to messages which do not pass the alignment test. The policy can be either to do nothing, quarantine emails, or reject them outright. The DMARC settings for a domain are in the DMARC record.

The DMARC record

The DMARC record is stored as a TXT record in the DNS for the domain used in the From field. It is always stored under the hostname "_dmarc". This means that if the From address was jill@example.com then the DMARC record, if it exists, will be stored at "_dmarc.example.com".

In the following example, the DMARC record has a policy of reject.

```
v=DMARC1; p=reject;
```

If the policy is "reject" or "quarantine" then recipient message filters may not place messages that fail DMARC tests in the inbox. DMARC policies can be a lot more complicated than this example. However, for deliverability purposes, being able to identify that a domain is protected by DMARC is sufficient.

DMARC does not positively influence deliverability in any meaningful way. That may change in the future, but currently you do not need to implement DMARC for deliverability purposes. However, DKIM alignment by itself can influence deliverability and should be implemented if possible.

If your organisation currently implements DMARC, you will need to liaise with the team responsible before you introduce any new method of sending messages on behalf of your domain name.

DMARC and deliverability

DMARC was never intended to be a deliverability friendly protocol. Its purpose is to cause messages which do not pass the DMARC policy to be filtered in some way. Even when properly deployed, DMARC with an enforcing policy can result in some legitimate messages not reaching inboxes. Why? Both SPF and DKIM can fail for legitimate reasons. For example, messages automatically forwarded to another destination after they have been received may cause the return-path to be rewritten, causing SPF to fall out of alignment for future DMARC tests. Any modification to a message, including a footer added by anti-virus software, will cause subsequent DKIM tests to fail.

DMARC allows for specific sub-domains to have different policies, allowing you to disable it for certain sub-domains. This is useful in situations where an organisation does not need to protect every mail stream. However, disabling DMARC is currently incompatible with the BIMI protocol.

Brand Indicators for Message Identification

Brand Indicators for Message Identification (BIMI) is an emerging protocol which displays a sender's brand image on compatible email clients. The current version of the protocol has a prerequisite that DMARC be enabled with an enforcing policy for both the base domain, and any sub-domain used in the From field of messages that are to display the brand image.

Organisations that wish to use BIMI should ensure that DMARC is professionally deployed. Professionally deployed and maintained, the potential for legitimate messages not reaching inboxes is typically reduced to statistically acceptable levels.

Monitoring

There are several ways a sender can check if their email authentication is configured correctly.

The simplest way to check your authentication settings is to send a test message to an address you control and look at the headers. Many mailbox providers add the *Authentication-Results* header, which contains information on how authentication was evaluated.

```
Authentication-Results: mta.example.com; spf=pass;
mta.example.com; dkim=pass;
dmarc=pass (p=reject dis=none);
```

The level of information provided in the Authentication-Results header depends on the individual mailbox provider.

If present, SPF results can also be reported in the Received-SPF header.

```
Received-SPF: Pass (sender SPF authorised)
identity=mailfrom; client-ip=192.168.55.60;
helo=mail.example.com; envelope-
from=test@example.com; receiver=jack@example.net
```

DMARC has a reporting capability which can tell you daily the SPF, DKIM, and DMARC success rates reported by participating receiving providers. Most large mailbox providers along with many smaller receivers support sending DMARC reports. The reporting will work with any policy, including one of "none". The raw reports are sent via email in Extensible Markup Language (XML) format. Therefore, reports are typically directed to a software or a service which parses the XML and displays the information in a more human readable form.

Google Postmaster Tools (see Chapter 3) will also report on the authentication metrics of messages delivered to Gmail.

This chapter covered email authentication, a collection of protocols that are used to prevent email fraud and sender impersonation but are also relevant to deliverability. FCrDNS is when the forward and reverse DNS of the sending MTA matches. An SPF record lists message sources allowed to send email on your behalf. DKIM digitally signs messages to identify any tampering. DMARC lets you tell mailbox providers what to do with email that does not pass either an SPF or DKIM test. BIMI is dependent on DMARC being enabled and allows a sender to surface their brand image on compatible email clients.

FCrDNS and SPF are a core requirement. Message filters like senders with "aligned" DKIM. DMARC is not currently required for deliverability but is for BIMI. If DMARC is implemented, you need to be aware of it before you make any changes to what sends messages from your domain. Authentication can be monitored in three ways: through the Authentication-Results and Receive-SPF messages headers, via DMARC reports, or using Google Postmaster Tools for Gmail-specific information.

Chapter 12
Conclusion – Putting the Jigsaw Together

At the beginning of this book, I described email deliverability as being like a jigsaw: all the pieces needed to come together for it to work. You know now what all those pieces look like and how to fit them together.

If you are all fired up to get started on improving your email deliverability, that's great. But… do not put the book down yet!

In the first edition of the book, I included a set of deliverability checklists which put all the best practices detailed in the book into categories. I also provided a facility for readers to get a PDF version of the checklists for their own use. The second edition of the book includes an accompanying website. This website has complementary tools, such as updated checklists available for download. Over time, the website will also have updated information in cases where something dramatically changes in a particular part of the industry.

You may also feel that you are not the person best placed to implement the changes needed to improve your deliverability. That is perfectly understandable, but remember you now have a common vocabulary and additional knowledge to help structure any remedial project or engagement. That puts you well ahead of where you were before you picked up this book.

Like Dorothy, you have seen behind the curtain, and you know that there is no wizard. The reality is that there is no quick fix to achieving a high level of email deliverability. It is all about taking measured steps and applying best current practices which are proportionate to how you use email.

As with anything else which is worth doing, email deliverability is worth doing properly.

Good luck.

Ken O'Driscoll
September 2023

Official Website

This book has an official website located at
https://emaildeliverabilityexplained.com/

Vendors and service providers

The first edition of the book listed many vendors and providers associated with the topics of the chapters. An updated list is available on the website.

Additional resources

The website will have supporting resources for both individual chapters and in general. For example, the updated deliverability checklists, based on those included with the first edition of the book, are now available.

Staying up to date

The email deliverability space is constantly changing. The website will keep track of the major changes.

A growing site

The website is intended to grow over time. So, if you are one of the early readers of this second edition then do not be shocked if the website looks a little sparse! The content and features of the site will mostly be driven by reader feedback. So, if there is some resource which you personally would like to see, let me know. Do not assume that someone else will think the same as you and tell me.

About the Author

Ken O'Driscoll lives in Dublin, Ireland with his wife Emily. He is the Head of Deliverability for Upland Software. Prior to that, he owned an email deliverability and DMARC consultancy practice.

Previously, Ken has held various senior positions in professional services companies, co-founded Ireland's first .EU ccTLD domain registrar, and was the Chief Technology Officer for a European mailbox provider.

This is the second edition of Ken's first book.

Contact Details

If you would like to get in touch, please use the contact details below. There are different contact points depending on your requirements.

Personal

My contact details and current social media handles are available on my personal website.

Website: https://kenodriscoll.com/

Book

If you would like to discuss any matters relating to the book, such as bulk orders, copyright, licensing or to report an error, please use the following email address.

Email: hello@emaildeliverabilityexplained.com

Index

Base64, file encoding ... 16
BIMI (Brand Indicators for Message Identification) ... 86
Bot clicks ... 33
Bounces
- deliverability, impact on ... 52
- different types of ... 49
- explained ... 49
- rate of, calculating ... 28
- suppression of ... 51

Captcha (use in sign-up forms) ... 53
Complaints
- abuse@ mailbox ... 30, 59
- feedback loops, use in reporting ... 25
- handling, importance of ... 55
- rate of, accuracy with ... 30
- rate of, calculating ... 30

Confirmed Opt-In (COI) ... 52
Content (filtering)
- checksums, use in ... 69
- explained ... 67
- links in messages, filtering of ... 69
- trigger words, continued use in B2B ... 67

DKIM (DomainKeys Identified Mail)
- alignment, advantage of ... 83
- explained ... 82
- feedback loops, connection with ... 83
- identifying mail streams, use in ... 23
- message header ... 83
- reputation, influence on ... 65

DKIM-Signature (message header) ... *See* DKIM, message header

DMARC (Domain-based Message Authentication, Reporting, and Conformance) ... 84
deliverability, influence on ... 85
DNS (Domain Name System)
A record ... 14
DKIM (TXT) record ... 83
DMARC (TXT) record ... 84
MX record ... 13, 14, 17, 80
PTR record ... 80
query limit (in SPF) ... 82
relationship with email delivery ... 13
reverse DNS ... *See* DNS, PTR record
service provider, need for reliability ... 59
SPF (TXT) record ... 80
TXT record ... 83, 84
Domain names
"fake" warming services, caution with ... 77
blocklists, listing by ... 37
choosing, care with ... 58
DKIM, use by ... 83
reputation ... 57
shared use domains, risks with ... 68

Email addresses
structure of ... 12
validating, existence of ... 43
validating, risks associated with ... 47
Email client ... *See* MUA
Email server ... *See* MTA
Engagement (filtering)
avoiding ... 75
explained ... 73
identifying ... 74
simulating, risks with ... 76
ESP (Email Service Provider) ... 24

False positives (with filters) ... 20
FCrDNS (Forward-confirmed reverse DNS) ... 79, 80, 87
Feedback Loops (FBLs) ... 25
Fuzzy checksum (in filtering) ... 69

Google Postmaster Tools....25, 65, 87

IMAP (Internet Message Access Protocol)....12, 17
Inbox placement, measuring....33
Internet Service Provider....*See* Mailbox Provider
IP addresses
  blocklists, listing by....37
  certification....65
  dedicated IPs
    number needed....62
    reputation, of....60
    warming, need for....62
  reputation
    definition....60
  shared IPs
    reputation, of....60
  SPF, use by....80

Mail streams....22
Mailbox Providers....24
MAPI (Messaging Application Programming Interface)....12, 17
Message filters....19
Message headers
  Authentication-Results....86, 87
  DKIM-Signature....83
  explained....14
  From
    5322.From, other name for....16
    DMARC, use of....84
    explained....15
  List-unsubscribe....54
  Received-SPF....86
  Return-path
    5321.MAILFROM, other name for....15
    bounces, use in....49
    explained....15
    SPF, use by....80
Metrics (deliverability related)....27
MIME (Multipurpose Internet Mail Extensions)....16, 17
MTA (Message Transfer Agent)....9
MUA (Mail User Agent)....12

Nocaptcha (use in sign-up forms) 54

Open rate (of an email campaign)
explained 32
reliability of 32
security filters, impact on 33

POP (Post Office Protocol) 12, 17
Pristine spam trap .... *See* Spam traps

Ramp plan .... *See* Warm-up plan
RBL (Realtime Block List) 37
of importance 40
Recycled spam trap .... *See* Spam traps
Return-path (email address) 15
bounces, connection with 49
SPF, connection with 80

Seed list 33
Smart Network Data Services (SNDS) 65
SMTP (Simple Mail Transfer Protocol)
explained 9
EXPN, command 43
MAIL FROM, command 10, 15, 44
open relays, problems with 11
STARTTLS, command 11
status codes 50
VRFY, command 43
Spam traps
blocklists, relationship with 37
explained 38
removal of 39
SpamAssassin 71
Spamhaus 41, 58
SPF (Sender Policy Framework)
DNS record 80
explained 80
Suppression list 51

TLS (Transport Layer Security) 11, 12, 17
Transactional messages 22, 26, 64

Typo spam trap .... *See* Spam traps

Unsubscribes
  honouring, importance of 54
  List-unsubscribe (message header) 54
  rate of, accuracy with 34
uuencode, file encoding 16

Warm-up plan 63

Printed in Great Britain
by Amazon

29975752R00062